"I'm excited to see a book  counseling with such wi practical and innovative that churches need to he rals, documentation, and other ethical concerns that can be e.. navigate in church settings."

Esther Smith, Director of Christian Trauma Counseling; author of *A Still and Quiet Mind*

"More and more churches are realizing the need to provide soul care to the people in their congregations. However, most pastors and church leaders are overwhelmed by the mere thought of the task. *Mobilizing Church-Based Counseling* is here to help. Brad Hambrick brings a wealth of insight and knowledge about people, churches, counseling, pastors, and the systems that are needed to bring these things together to offer helpful, biblical, sustainable care through lay counseling ministries. Whether you are looking to start a counseling ministry, seeking wisdom to sustain a struggling counseling ministry, or building on an existing one, *Mobilizing* will help."

Curtis Solomon, Executive Director, Biblical Counseling Coalition; program coordinator for biblical counseling, Boyce College

"Many churches love the idea of being a place of care, but they are sobered by the possibility of hurting rather than helping. Strong pastoral counseling, lay counseling, and counseling groups truly are difficult to do in an organized and effective way. Brad has done church leaders a real service by offering a realistic template for providing relational ministry wisely and well for the problems of life. Highly recommend."

Michael Gembola, Director, Blue Ridge Christian Counseling; author of *Anxious about Decisions*

"Many churches recognize the need to provide a faithful counseling ministry but simply do not know how to start or what to do. *Mobilizing Church-Based Counseling* addresses these challenges with wisdom, guidance, and practical plans for implementation. Thankfully, this book does not advocate a one-size-fits-all approach but provides adaptable models to choose from. Brad Hambrick is both a seminary professor and a local church counselor and is the perfect person to author this much-needed book."

Daniel L. Akin, President, Southeastern Baptist Theological Seminary

"*Mobilizing Church-Based Counseling* is the most practical thing I have ever read. Brad's years of experience navigating the problems churches face creating structures is pervasively evident. If you want a *sustainable* plan for the most common counseling challenges churches encounter, you couldn't do better than this book (and you might want to get a dozen copies to share)."

J. Alasdair Groves, Executive Director, CCEF (Christian Counseling & Educational Foundation); coauthor of *Untangling Emotions*

"In *Mobilizing Church-Based Counseling*, Brad comes alongside you and explains exactly what you need to know to start a church-based counseling ministry. He's anticipated your questions and highlights the information that's most important for *you*, given your church's goals and resources. Reading the book is almost like talking with Brad. *Mobilizing* is an easy-to-understand guide that you'll refer to often."

Sam Hodges IV, President, Church Initiative (GriefShare and DivorceCare)

MOBILIZING CHURCH-BASED COUNSELING

MODELS FOR SUSTAINABLE CHURCH-BASED CARE

Brad Hambrick

New
Growth
Press

newgrowthpress.com

New Growth Press, Greensboro, NC 27401
newgrowthpress.com
Copyright © 2023 by Brad Hambrick

All rights reserved. No part of this publication may be reproduced, stored in a retrieval system, or transmitted in any form by any means, electronic, mechanical, photocopy, recording, or otherwise, without the prior permission of the publisher, except as provided by USA copyright law.

Unless otherwise noted, Scripture quotations are taken from the ESV® Bible (the Holy Bible, English Standard Version®). ESV® Text Edition: 2016. Copyright © 2001 by Crossway Bibles, a publishing ministry of Good News Publishers. The ESV® text has been reproduced in cooperation with and by permission of Good News Publishers. Unauthorized reproduction of this publication is prohibited. All rights reserved.

Scripture quotations marked NIV are taken from the Holy Bible, New International Version®, NIV®. Copyright © 1973, 1978, 1984, 2011 by Biblica, Inc.™ Used by permission of Zondervan. All rights reserved worldwide. www.zondervan.com. The "NIV" and "New International Version" are trademarks registered in the United States Patent and Trademark Office by Biblica, Inc.™

Cover Design: Faceout Books, faceoutstudio.com
Interior Typesetting and eBook: Lisa Parnell, lparnellbookservices.com

ISBN: 978-1-64507-329-1 (Print)
ISBN: 978-1-64507-330-7 (eBook)

Library of Congress Cataloging-in-Publication Data on file

Printed in the United States of America

30 29 28 27 26 25 24 23   1 2 3 4 5

CONTENTS

FOREWORD

Around The Summit Church, we have a handful of sayings we call "plumb lines"—short, pithy statements that help us direct and measure our ministry. Brick masons use plumb lines to build a wall straight and true. Our plumb lines help us build God's church the same way.

One of my favorite Summit plumb lines is this: "Show your work and let others copy your paper." No, this isn't a statement endorsing plagiarism. It captures our desire to do our ministry work with intentionally open hands. What we do in *our* church, for *our* people, in *our* context—and this local context is always paramount—just might be fruitful for other churches and people and contexts.

Multiplication is at the heart of the Great Commission. We are not only supposed to do our work well, but to teach others to do it also—sometimes better than we do it. We are called not only to be successful, but to reproduce. If God prospers you at something, take that extra time to write down the secrets of your success so that others can do it too. Though that might feel at times like a cumbersome process, the benefit it brings to others will more than make up for any inconvenience. Proverbs 12:27 (NIV) says, "The lazy do not roast any game, but the diligent feed on the riches of the hunt." Making the kill is only half the success of hunting; dress the game and get it into the refrigerator so that others can feast on your success later!

When I think of people who do this well, at the top of the list is our pastor of counseling, Brad Hambrick. I know few people with the wisdom and insight he possesses. But Brad is also a master at showing his work. Which is precisely what he does here, in *Mobilizing Church-Based Counseling* and *Facilitating Counseling Groups*. He's showing his work, letting your church replicate two highly effective, much-needed ministries.

G4 (support and recovery groups) and Gospel-Centered Marriage (our premarital counseling ministry) are two ministries that have mobilized our members and served the Summit well for over a decade. I cannot imagine the life of The Summit Church without them. Or, maybe more honestly, I don't want to.

I've seen more lives changed as a result of these ministries than I can recount. But it's not the result of Brad's magical hand. It's the result of a gospel-driven process—one that your church can and should learn.

We end every worship service at the Summit with a simple commission: "You are sent." It's a reminder that every member of our church has been sent by God to bring God's healing and hope into the world.

That's my dream for these books, too. We are sending them out into the world to bring God's healing and hope—beginning, perhaps today, with your church.

J. D. Greear
Lead Pastor, The Summit Church, Raleigh-Durham, NC

Preface

HOW TO READ AND IMPLEMENT
MOBILIZING

In the pages ahead you (the reader) and I (the author) will be taking a journey together. At the same time, you and your church will be exploring the possibility of mobilizing a church-based counseling ministry. This preface is meant to help you synchronize these two journeys. Since starting a counseling ministry is a novel endeavor for most churches, I want to help you and your church's leadership to understand how to avoid three common mistakes that can create frustration on the road ahead.

First, read the entirety of *Mobilizing* before you start trying to implement anything or conversing with your potential first-generation lay leaders. Don't be like me with a new piece of IKEA furniture. I buy it, get excited, start assembling pieces as soon as I open the box, and then, when I get to what I realize is step 7, I discover I misunderstood something. At that point I'm frustrated about the work I need to undo and redo. Please get the complete picture before you start. It is far easier to correct a mistake in assembling a piece of prefabricated furniture than it is to retrieve inaccurate information about your new counseling ministry that is spreading among excited church members because of a too-early, inaccurate conversation.

Second, when you introduce this book to your pastor(s)—ideally after you've finished reading it yourself—recommend that they read chapter 19 first. That chapter contains the information most pastors want to know when vetting the potential of launching a counseling ministry. A shared discussion of chapter 19 will demonstrate that you're familiar enough with the content of this book to merit the trust of your pastor and alleviate the most common apprehensions. As we'll discuss in chapters 7 and 8, many prospective counseling ministries have never emerged because of their proponents' inability to navigate concerns of liability, sustainability, and "fit" with other church ministries.

Third, realize that *Mobilizing* goes out of its way to give your church as much freedom as possible in how you implement the two lay counseling ministry models it introduces. This freedom is likely to be simultaneously refreshing and frustrating. If something is important, *Mobilizing* strives to be clear. If something can vary from church to church—based on size, denomination, church doctrine, church polity, leadership preferences, or other factors—it strives to be non-restrictive. As you move toward a launch plan in chapters 16 and 17, you'll learn how to forge a relationship with a local professional counselor to ensure you steward this freedom wisely.

Now, with that bit of guidance under your belt, let's begin!

An Introduction
to Church-Based Counseling

Chapter 1

YOU WANT TO DO A GOOD THING: LET'S DO IT WELL!

The fact that you're reading this book means you want to do a very good thing! You want to help hurting people. You want to mobilize your church to be a source of care for its members and community. You want to point people to the hope of Christ amid their hardships.

You want to invite people into a community of care where everyone acknowledges their brokenness (Psalm 34:18) and seeks redemption together (Galatians 3:13). You want to break the stigma of counseling and cultivate a community where it's okay to be a work in process (Hebrews 4:15–16).

You want to make the church a more authentic place. You want to deepen surface-level prayer requests and head-knowledge Bible studies. You want to find out what would happen if we all quit "playing church" and opened ourselves up to the possibility of God changing our personal, emotional, and relational lives. You want your church to be a conduit through which people experience all that God wants to be and do in their lives (Acts 3:20).

These are all good things, and my prayer is that this book will help you bring them about through the ministry models we'll discuss.

Because these are all such good things, we are left asking questions. *Why aren't there more church-based counseling models? Why aren't there a litany of ministries churches can adapt and implement to fulfill these good objectives? Why do church leaders often get nervous about starting a counseling ministry when we just want to help people?*

These are important questions, and there are important questions behind these questions. This book is about helping you understand all of them so that you can do the good thing you want to do *with excellence*.

That word *excellence* may move you from excitement to angst as you wonder, *What if I've never done anything like start a counseling ministry before?* That's a healthy concern—it reveals humility—and we'll take this concern seriously. This book assumes that you are a lay volunteer without advanced training in counseling. In the pages ahead, you'll learn how to secure experienced supervision, to honor the information disclosed in this new ministry, and to build a team so that you don't have to carry these responsibilities alone. Ironically, starting this ministry requires the same courage to face uncertainty that participants in your counseling ministry will show when they first reach out for help. Pay attention to the unsettledness you feel; navigating this experience will help you care for others.

With these things in mind, know the underlying premise of this book is this: *the more important something is, the more important it is to do it well and the more dangerous it is to do it sloppily.* Because a counseling ministry will invite people to be vulnerable with the most sensitive parts of their lives, it will—for better or worse—have immense influence. With great influence comes great responsibility.

But doing a lay counseling ministry well doesn't necessarily mean mimicking professional models (i.e., intake forms, case notes, meeting by appointment, creating an individualized treatment plan, etc.). In a local church, it means creating a ministry that fits within a church context and which can be implemented by lay volunteers. In light of this understanding of "good," *Mobilizing* focuses on helping you launch two specific lay counseling ministries: a group-based model

3

called G4 and a mentoring model called GCM. We'll define G4 and GCM in chapters 3 through 6, but for now, you need to understand these counseling ministries were designed to have three key features. These features are:

1. *Compatibility with the local church*: G4 and GCM are designed to be led effectively by laypeople in your church and to fit within the rhythms of a leader's schedule and a church's structures.
2. *Wisdom about issues of liability*: G4 and GCM are designed with the informed consent and the ethical consideration needed for a moderately formal, lay-based ministry.
3. *Sustainability for your volunteers*: G4 and GCM are designed with a recognition that the longevity of your mentors and group leaders is essential to an effective lay-based ministry.

In the pages ahead, the significance of these three features will become increasingly clear to you. You will see how these features are woven into almost every facet of G4 and GCM. Being able to highlight these features will bring comfort to your church leadership, potential volunteers, and growing list of community partners. These features reveal that you have more than good intentions; you have a solid plan that allows you to care well for people in difficult situations.

You will also realize that "creating a counseling ministry" is different from "training counselors." Training helpers is only one part of the process and is *not* the first thing to be done. That's why we will take the following three-tiered approach:

- Section one clarifies *common points of confusion* about church-based counseling.
- Section two provides guidance on the neglected subject of *counseling ethics* in lay-based care models.
- Section three lays out a *launch plan* for G4 and GCM.

Until these things are well understood, it would be unwise to move toward vetting and training potential lay leaders for these ministries. To be ready to care for these leaders, you and your church leadership need to be clear about what you're inviting them to participate in.

If you are ready to take this journey in a way that values quality more than expediency (that is, doing things well more than doing things quickly), this book will be satisfying for you.

Chapter 2

WHO ARE YOU: WHO WAS *MOBILIZING* WRITTEN TO EQUIP?

Who are *you*? My name is Brad. I grew up in Kentucky, currently live in North Carolina, enjoy coaching Little League baseball, and don't take time to go fishing as often as I should. You may have guessed that is not the kind of "Who are you?" information my opening question is trying to elicit.

My question would better be written, Who is the "*you*" that *Mobilizing* is speaking to? What role, at your church, does this book presume you (the reader) are in? The "*you*" in this book is the person who will oversee G4 and/or GCM.

You are probably a layperson because most churches don't have a staff position to oversee these ministries—or at least don't start with one. You are the kind of person who takes the initiative of a first-generation leader; that is, someone who is willing to put in the sweat equity to start a ministry that doesn't currently exist at your church. However, if you are both the first person to read this book at your church and the pastor, the "*you*" is the kind of volunteer you are looking for to champion this ministry in your church.

But don't take this to mean you should be a lone ranger. The accompanying graphic portrays how you'll relate to the pastoral leaders in your church and those you recruit to lead in these ministries. While it conveys whom you report to and who reports to you, it is more than an organizational chart. It visualizes *who* will be involved with you (building a team), *what* each person needs to read (training), and *why* they need to read that resource (each person's role).

As you are getting started, if possible, you want one or more of the pastoral staff at your church to read *Mobilizing* with you and become involved in the ministry development plans. It is important for church leadership to be aware of what kind of ministries G4 and GCM are so that they talk about these ministries accurately, even in the early stages of ministry planning.

Who? Church Leadership
What? *Mobilizing*
Why? Understand & Support

Who? *You*
What? *Mobilizing*
Why? Implement & Oversee

Who? G4 and GCM Leaders
What? *Facilitating* for G4 or GCM Mentor Training Manual
Why? Lead Groups & Mentor

To employ a flight metaphor, *Mobilizing* is the book that helps you build a "counseling airport" with the necessary runways, traffic control tower, and communication protocols. If you only have an airport, what's missing? Pilots and passengers. Who are they?

- Pilots—G4 group leaders and GCM mentors
- Passengers—Those being served in these ministries

Mobilizing is the book that helps you build the airport (because, without an airport, pilots, planes, and passengers never get off the ground). As such, *Mobilizing* contains the content you and church leadership need to discuss when launching or expanding G4 and GCM. *Facilitating Counseling Groups[1]* will help you train G4 "pilots," as will the *Mentor Training Manual* for GCM.[2] These resources equip and orient lay leaders to their role in G4 or GCM. As you're beginning to see, *Mobilizing* provides a layered model of lay counseling. G4

---

1. *Facilitating Counseling Groups: A Leader's Guide for Group-Based Counseling Ministry* (Greensboro, NC: New Growth Press, 2023).
2. The GCM *Mentor Training Manual* and accompanying mentor training video are available at bradhambrick.com/gcm.

and GCM are more than friend, less than professional, and different from a pastor. Each of these roles is good—friends, professionals, and pastors—but a church-based counseling ministry differs from each. In the pages ahead, you'll learn why and how to communicate these differences.

While you will likely also lead a G4 group or be a GCM mentor (at least initially), as you read *Mobilizing*, think of yourself as being in the traffic control tower. At this phase of development, you are working with the airport overseers (church leadership) to understand the design and layout of this ministry.

When the preparatory work is done, you will begin vetting and equipping prospective pilots (lay leaders) for their work. As these ministries grow, you'll see G4 and GCM leaders emerge who are passionate about these ministries and can help share your oversight role. They will read *Mobilizing* and begin to help you ensure that G4 and GCM operate with excellence. This lessens the load you carry.

This chapter may feel daunting. In effect, chapter 2 narrated a marathon in the word count of a sprint. It overviewed the full journey of this book. Anytime you look at a whole journey, it has the tendency to feel overwhelming.

You are now ready (maybe past ready) to ask, What are these G4 and GCM ministries that *Mobilizing* is going to teach me to implement at my church? What do they look like? What's their core DNA? How would I tell people what I want to do with what I'm learning?

Chapter 3

WHAT IS G4?

In chapter one, I told you this book would equip your church to launch two specific lay counseling models, G4 and GCM. You know that G4 is a group-based model and GCM is a mentoring ministry. In the next four chapters, I will define and then illustrate each ministry.

WHAT IS G4?

G4 is a group-based counseling ministry that provides a context for participants to invest a season of their lives in overcoming a life-dominating struggle of sin or suffering. Most G4 groups utilize a subject specific curriculum (addiction, depression, eating disorders, grief, trauma, etc.) built around one of two nine-step models of sanctification.

The goal of G4 is to see participants graduate back into the general discipleship ministries of the church, freer from their struggle and with a clearer picture of what it means for believers to support one another as the gospel transforms the most difficult parts of our lives.

WHY THE NAME "G4"?

"G" is for gospel. Too often in counseling groups, our struggle becomes our identity. The longer someone is in a group, the more their identity becomes "addict," "depressed," or "divorced." G4 provides the benefit of a place to be known without the detriment of cultivating a struggle-based identity.

We place the "G" at the front of G4 to serve as a reminder that our identity is found not in our struggle but in our Savior—Jesus Christ. Yes, we struggle. Yes, it is freeing to have a place to be honest about that. But, no, our struggles do not define us. Through the gospel God tells us who we are and makes us more and more into the people he created us to be.

The number "**4**" represents the four types of groups that can be housed within a G4 ministry. Not all counseling groups are the same. If you put one type of group at the forefront of your ministry, it inadvertently communicates a limited scope. For instance, if you label your ministry as a *recovery ministry*, it gives the perception that it only deals with addiction. The name G4 was chosen to prevent the ministry from being identified with any one niche of struggles.

A benign name like G4 also destigmatizes a ministry that might otherwise be hard to talk about. Participants can say, "I've got a G4 meeting tonight," without disclosing more than they intend. A pastor preaching on purity can talk about the G4 groups at church without trying to define sexual addiction. A ministry that depends on word of mouth needs to be easy to talk about, and "G4" is short, simple, and neutral.

Here is a basic definition for each of the four types of groups that can exist within G4:

1. *Recovery Groups* are for addressing destructive, habituated life patterns, such as substance abuse, chemical addiction, or behavioral addictions (e.g., pornography or gambling).
2. *Process Groups* are for decreasing the disruption caused by difficult experiences or "sticky" emotions. They might address trauma or the aftermath of destructive relationships.
3. *Support Groups* are for mutual encouragement as participants persevere through difficult experiences that endure for an indefinite period of time, such as divorce, depression, or grief.
4. *Therapeutic Educational Groups* provide a better understanding of challenges that are often misunderstood and might provide

a holistic Christian perspective on mental health or identify common challenges for blended families.

A G4 ministry does not need to have a group of each type to be called G4. For instance, if a church only has recovery groups and process groups in its offerings, it would still be called G4.

The types of groups are not as distinct as they initially appear. All groups, to some degree, offer therapeutic education. Every type of group involves processing difficult experiences together. It is not important that every group fit neatly into one of the four types. It is important, however, to be clear about what distinguishes G4 groups from general discipleship ministries of your church.

TWO NINE-STEP MODELS

The gospel offers hope for both sin and suffering—the bad things we do and the painful things we experience. But the gospel speaks to sin and suffering differently; it offers forgiveness and freedom for sin and comfort and hope for suffering. That is why G4 has two nine-step models.

Because every person is both a sinner and a sufferer, we all need both. But our struggles usually fall more into one category than the other. Anger and addiction are predominantly, though not exclusively, responsibility-based struggles (sin). They emanate from our choices and values. You will notice that the phrases "responsibility-based" and "sin-based" are used interchangeably. When G4 uses a sin-based curriculum, it is because the participant bears responsibility for having caused the life struggle. By contrast, grief and trauma are things that happen to us (suffering). In using G4, a leader becomes ambidextrous in discerning and applying the best fit gospel-care for an individual's most pressing need.

We do not believe there is any magic in these nine-step models of G4. We *do* believe these steps capture the major movements of the gospel, in slow motion, as they are applied with a concentrated focus toward a particular life struggle such as anxiety, purity, or betrayal.

G4's Nine Steps for Sin-Based Struggles[1]

Step 1: ADMIT I have a struggle I cannot overcome without God (John 15:5). We should not assume that everyone who comes to group and is frustrated by the consequences of their choices is ready to change. In step 1, G4 seeks to garner a commitment to change and introduces God as central to the work ahead.

Step 2: ACKNOWLEDGE the breadth and impact of my sin. We should not assume that everyone who wants to change is being honest with themselves about how much change is needed (Psalm 36:1–3; James 1:8). In step 2, G4 walks the participant through the process of identifying the pervasiveness and severity of their struggle (Luke 14:28–29).

Step 3: UNDERSTAND the origin, motive, and history of my sin. We are often confused by the question, Why do I keep doing this if I know it's disrupting my life? In step 3, G4 helps participants identify the motives undergirding their sin patterns (Luke 6:45) and introduces a more holistic understanding of what it means to have a fallen human nature (Romans 3:10–18).

Step 4: REPENT TO GOD for how my sin replaced and misrepresented him. Repentance is more than a sense of remorse (2 Corinthians 7:10–11). In step 4, G4 introduces the idea that substantive change begins with embracing the gospel and submitting our lives to the Lordship of Christ (Luke 9:23–26). This step undermines the pride that leads us to resist help and the belief that just trying harder will work this time (Matthew 23:26–28).

Step 5: CONFESS TO THOSE AFFECTED for harm done and seek to make amends. Privacy fuels sin and kills change (Proverbs 28:13). Transparency fuels change and kills sin (James 5:16). In step 5, G4 introduces the idea that God created us to live in community and our sin tempts us to withdraw. Change means we become more honest and authentic, not better at hiding.

---

1. A video-based teaching of these nine steps is available as a small group study at bradhambrick.com/G4SinModel. This video-based teaching is designed for two purposes. First, it orients new G4 participants to the big picture of their journey. Secondly, it can be used as a small group study in your church after your pastor preaches on an emotionally weighty subject like addiction, sexual purity, or anger to raise awareness for your G4 ministry.

Step 6: RESTRUCTURE MY LIFE to rely on God's grace and Word to transform my life. Substantive change doesn't happen by accident. It happens with intentionality. In step 6, G4 provides a variety of strategies for change tailored to each curriculum's life struggle (Ephesians 4:20–31). This step provides the practical guidance most people want when they seek counseling.

Step 7: IMPLEMENT the new structure pervasively with humility and flexibility. A famous boxer once said, "Everyone has a plan until they get punched in the mouth." Life never goes according to our plans. Step 7 invites participants to review and revise how they are implementing the strategies from step 6, based on what is and is not effective (Luke 4:13).

Step 8: PERSEVERE in the new life and identity to which God has called me. Change is like wet cement; it becomes solid over time (Philippians 1:6). Step 8 calls the participant to allow their newfound change to solidify as they begin to make plans to graduate from their G4 group into the discipleship ministries of their church.

Step 9: STEWARD all of my life for God's glory. The Christian life is about more than the absence of particular sins; it is about fulfilling a purpose (Matthew 22:37–40). In step 9, participants are invited to ask, "What does God have for me next?" so that their G4 graduation is an opportunity for the group to commission their friend toward that calling.

Each G4 series curriculum takes one life struggle (e.g., substance abuse, sexual addiction, disordered eating) and goes into detail on each step for that struggle. The curriculum provides assessments, Bible studies, strategies for change, and educational content to help the participant successfully accomplish that step.

Perhaps you've had the opportunity to talk with someone for whom the twelve steps of Alcoholics Anonymous were central in their overcoming addiction. You probably noticed how naturally they began to use the twelve steps as a grid for navigating life. They couldn't help but share the twelve steps as they told their story. Similarly, the goal of the nine gospel-centered steps of G4 is for a clear understanding of the gospel to become the natural grid participants use to navigate life and talk about the major changes in their lives.

Before we walk through the nine steps for sufferers, let's admit that, historically, the church has been better at applying the gospel to sin-based struggles than suffering-based struggles. There is a reason for this. We get saved from sin; we don't get saved from suffering (at least not on this side of heaven). So, while it's understandable that we apply the gospel more effectively to sin-based struggles, we should be equally effective in applying it to suffering. With that in mind, let's explore what the gospel offers those who suffer.

G4's Nine Steps for Suffering-Based Struggles[2]

Step 1: PREPARE yourself physically, emotionally, and spiritually to face your suffering. People reach out for help amid suffering when they are hope-depleted. They are weary and the journey is long (Matthew 11:28, 2 Corinthians 4:16). In step 1, G4 helps the participant identify the pivotal choices that will enable them to persevere through the work ahead.

Step 2: ACKNOWLEDGE the specific history and realness of my suffering. We often minimize and misname our suffering, thinking that will help us overcome it. We tell ourselves, "The abuse wasn't that bad," or, "The car wreck wasn't really traumatic." In step 2, G4 walks the participant through the process of rightly naming their experiences of suffering (Ezekiel 34:1–10).

Step 3: UNDERSTAND the impact of my suffering. Suffering is not just "then and there." It doesn't stay in the past; suffering has an impact on the here and now (Isaiah 42:3). In step 3, G4 helps the participant articulate and gauge the current impact of their suffering.

Step 4: LEARN MY SUFFERING STORY, which I use to make sense of my experience. Yesterday is the preface to today. Past events

---

2. A video-based teaching of these nine steps is available as a small group study at bradhambrick.com/G4SufferingModel. This video-based teaching is designed for two purposes. First, it orients new G4 participants to the big picture of their step work journey. Second, it can be used as a small group study for your church after your pastor preaches on an emotionally weighty subject like trauma, betrayal, or grief to raise awareness for your G4 ministry.

shape our present identity. Suffering affects how we tell our stories and understand our lives (Psalm 44:22–26). In step 4, G4 helps participants recognize and articulate the destructive scripts they've taken from their suffering—scripts that often disrupt their lives as much as the original experience of suffering did.

Step 5: MOURN the wrongness of what happened and receive God's comfort. Suffering isn't just hard; it reveals that the world is not as God intended. Suffering is a reason to mourn (Romans 8:22–23). In step 5, G4 invites participants to mourn the hardness of what they learned in steps 2 and 3, without the shame they felt from the false messages revealed in step 4.

Step 6: LEARN MY GOSPEL STORY by which God gives meaning to my experience. Truth doesn't make hard times easy (John 16:33). Truth *does* give meaning to struggles that seem futile (Hebrews 12:2–3). In step 6, G4 helps participants reinterpret the destructive scripts from step 4 in ways that show God's care for them and give meaning to their hardship.

Step 7: IDENTIFY GOALS that allow me to combat the impact of my suffering. Even when we reduce the sense of meaninglessness suffering brings, suffering is still hard (2 Corinthians 1:8–9); it affects other aspects of our lives (Psalm 102:3–11). In step 7, G4 helps participants identify ways to reduce the impacts identified in step 3.

Step 8: PERSEVERE in the new life and identity to which God has called me. This step closely mirrors step 8 in the sin-based curriculum. It is a time for the participant to solidify the change they've experienced and prepare to wisely graduate from G4.

Step 9: STEWARD all of my life for God's glory. This step also mirrors step 9 in the sin-based curriculum. We always want people to graduate from G4 with a sense of anticipation for what God has in store for them in the next season of their lives.

After reading through these two nine-step models, you should be able to see more clearly how the gospel speaks to sin and suffering differently. The Bible is our guide for both, and Jesus's work on the cross to counter the effects of the fall is central. But when someone's struggle is rooted in their beliefs, values, and choices, their curriculum will be sin-based. When their struggle is rooted in things that have happened to them, they will participate in a suffering-based curriculum.

Although these nine-step models were created to be used in G4 groups, the G4 ministry was also designed to house groups that do not use our standard nine-step curriculums. Many excellent counseling group curriculums have been written by faithful Christian authors. Unfortunately, while churches may have appreciated the content, they often weren't sure where or how these resources fit within their existing ministry offerings. G4 was intentionally designed so that churches would have an intuitive home for these curriculums. How this works is answered in detail in chapter 15 of *Facilitating Counseling Groups*, the sequel to this book.

SEVEN CORE VALUES OF G4

In a large G4 ministry, there are multiple groups, each focused on a different life struggle—yet a unity of purpose runs through all the groups. A consistent culture among G4 groups is maintained by adhering to seven core values. These values undergird all that happens in the counseling ministry and are implemented by leaders of each group. These values are described in greater detail in chapter 4 of *Facilitating*. These values are simply listed here so that you and your church leadership are reminded of the values that guide a G4 ministry:

1. G4 curriculums are Bible-based and gospel-centered.
2. G4 recognizes the difference between sin and suffering.
3. G4 groups are built on honesty and transparency.
4. G4 upholds confidentiality.
5. G4 avoids creating struggle-based identity.
6. G4 blends discipleship, accountability, and a guided process.
7. G4 transitions into the church's discipleship ministries.

Now that we've defined G4, the natural follow-up question is, What does G4 look like? That's what we'll describe in the next chapter. We'll provide this picture in the form of a story, which will help flesh out the framework of G4 that we've outlined in this chapter.

Chapter 4

A GRASSROOTS LAUNCH STORY FOR G4

This is a story of G4 launching at an average-sized church (i.e., non-mega church). It assumes G4 is being launched by someone like you, a layperson with a burden for their church to have a counseling ministry. This is important because most ministries that get off the ground need to be able to start at the grassroots level; that is, without paid staff to oversee their development.

If you are at a large church, your process will likely be more large scale than grassroots. Chapter 16 provides a launch model for a collection of groups in a cohesive G4 ministry. However, this story illustrates the multiplication qualities of G4 that allow this ministry to launch at a church of any size and expand to meet emerging needs.

The remainder of this chapter tells a fictional story depicting what it might look like for G4 to grow organically at your church. Consider this story to be primarily vision-casting. It is not giving you a step-by-step process of how G4 *should* start, but is instead giving you possibilities for the ways G4 *could* start and grow. As the story unfolds, you'll see some common challenges that emerge within an organic approach so that you can begin to prepare for them.

THE STORY BEGINS

Trevor and Connor were well-respected young men in the church. They met weekly for breakfast, often admitting to each other their shared struggle with pornography. They decided they needed to get serious about changing. After some research on possible resources, they decided they liked the G4 *False Love* study (bradhambrick.com/falselove) because it had clear steps and a workbook, was biblically based, and offered the option of listening to the pastoral counselor who wrote the material via video or podcast.

After they got a few steps in, they realized there was a corresponding study for their wives called *True Betrayal* (bradhambrick.com/truebetrayal). They mentioned it to their wives, Caitlyn and Molly, who decided this would be good for them to study together. They'd always wished there was something that helped them process the hurt they felt. The guys started to have victory over pornography, and their wives felt like there was finally something to help them.

As Trevor and Connor worked through their study, they realized that they couldn't be the only guys at the church who needed this. Mustering up some courage, Trevor talked with Pastor Philip, explained how he and Connor had been meeting, and offered, "If you come across any guys who need it, we'd be willing to start a G4 group on Tuesday nights."

Pastor Philip knew of several men who had confided a struggle with pornography, so he called to let them know about the new group. Connor had a similar conversation with Xavier, who oversaw the men's ministry at church, and after he mentioned the new group at their next men's gathering, a couple more guys got connected. Because G4 groups are open—meaning participants can join at any time and graduate when they're ready—the group was always ready to welcome new members. Soon, there were regularly eight to ten guys meeting on Tuesday nights to work through the G4 *False Love* curriculum.

When Caitlyn saw that the men's group was taking off, she realized many of these guys were married and their wives were hurting in silence as much as she had been. Molly wasn't comfortable leading a group, so Caitlyn started solo. But soon, the women's betrayal group averaged ten ladies each week, and the men's group multiplied into two groups of twelve to fourteen each, including guys from three other churches.

As several of the ladies got close to finishing their work through the *True Betrayal* curriculum, they started to look though the other G4 resources. Lesley was excited to find a study on depression-anxiety. She had always felt shame because of her struggle with these emotions. When she graduated from the betrayal group, the group commissioned her to start a depression-anxiety group. This group was filled almost immediately following an announcement from Pastor Philip and a blurb on the women's ministry monthly email.

Jae from the men's purity group had a similar experience. He was a law enforcement officer and had a buddy who was an EMT. In connection with their work, they knew lots of colleagues who saw gruesome stuff on a regular basis. They often talked about how seeing that stuff "messes with you and sticks in your mind." Jae saw there was a G4 trauma curriculum and thought that offering it would be a great way to care for his first responder coworkers.

Jae started the group and talked to the chaplains at the fire department, police station, and local veteran's hospital. Slowly that group increased to five or six participants. It didn't grow as fast, but the bond and depth of relationship in this group may have been stronger than in any of the others. It was also the first group to begin having several nonbelievers faithfully attend.

Eighteen months after Trevor and Connor started the first group, there were five groups: two men's purity, a women's betrayal, a women's depression-anxiety, and a coed trauma group for first responders and veterans. There another generation was starting to graduate, and several of them were interested in starting new groups.

Somehow, Trevor and Caitlyn became the de facto leaders for this burgeoning network of G4 groups, but it was starting to get overwhelming. It was hard to keep track of which group was meeting where for what and when. They could tell each group was starting to develop its own culture, which was fine for now, but if they went from five groups to ten groups, these differences would increase and make it harder to effectively communicate with new participants and the wider church what to expect from G4. They could also see that group leaders were getting tired and starting to feel isolated.

Trevor and Caitlyn called a meeting with Pastor Philip and the other G4 leaders—both active leaders and those thinking about launching new groups. They celebrated all that God had done in the last two years and acknowledged the things that were becoming difficult. Someone brought up the idea of shifting from individual G4 groups to a consolidated G4 ministry that would meet on one night of the week.

They realized this transition would involve more than having a couple of groups change which night of the week they met and reserving the education wing of the church building on Thursday nights. It would mean coordinating a new large group time that would serve as an opening ceremony for the night of G4. While this new large group time would allow G4 leaders to shape a more consistent G4 culture, someone would have to plan for and lead this time. *And what about snacks?* The same was true for the new post-group leader debrief, which would ease leaders' sense of fatigue and isolation. This would help leaders, but it would also require planning.

Clearly, the ministry needed a coordinator for the whole thing—a G4 director. Initially, everyone thought Trevor would be the natural person to take on this role. After all, he started the first G4 group and called this meeting. But Trevor wasn't very good at speaking in front of large groups, didn't like administration, couldn't add anything else to his schedule, and didn't want to give up leading his men's purity group. After a bit of discussion, they decided Mateo was the best person for this role. Mateo had been Trevor's co-leader for the last year. He was comfortable leading events from a stage and had a good mind for systems. He wanted to do more with G4 but didn't want to lead his own group.

Mateo joined a cohort of leaders from other churches that were exploring the idea of launching G4, and they studied together *Mobilizing* and *Facilitating*, the training for new G4 leaders.[1] This gave him the opportunity to learn alongside people who were in the early stages of launching a G4 ministry. Mateo learned how to fill his role as G4 director in ways that cared for his leaders and increased G4's

---

1. Information about upcoming training events can be found at bradhambrick.com/events.

impact in the community. Mateo's church agreed to pay his cohort fee as a sign of its commitment to this growing ministry.

Once the ministry had been consolidated, communicating clearly about what G4 offered—as well as where and when—became so much easier. Now anyone who asked about G4 could be told the following:

> G4 meets in the education wing of the church on Thursday nights from 6:30 until 8:00 p.m. There are a variety of groups, all led by laypeople. You can check the church website[2] to find a list of active groups.

They made up a few flyers to give to area counselors and Christian business owners who would put them in their waiting rooms to raise awareness for the ministry.

The large group time helped with the assimilation of new participants and gave a natural place for emphasizing the seven core values of G4. Periodically discussing things like confidentiality, transparency, and G4's relationship to the church's discipleship ministries helped keep all the groups aligned on these values that shape the culture of each group.

Mateo set a schedule for the leader debrief. It met for thirty minutes at the end of group time. They rotated through four topics each month: (a) testimonies and celebration of things happening in groups; (b) an outside speaker to teach on a relevant topic; (c) food and fellowship; and (d) a Q&A time with leaders to answer emerging questions and suggest topics for future guest speakers. The leaders enjoyed getting to know one another and being sharpened for their ministry. Speakers included a social worker, a psychiatrist, an ER nurse, and a nutritionist.

The momentum led to several new groups. Volunteers gained peace of mind knowing that Mateo could reach out to professionals for help if something came up in one of their groups. This gave them confidence that G4 would respond to the hard situations effectively. The Christian professionals enjoyed getting to use their expertise to strengthen a church's ministry without adding more direct care hours

---

2. For a sample of how you might lay out this page, you can visit summitchurch.com/G4.

to their workweek. Attending G4 group sessions increased these professionals' willingness to recommend G4 to their clients.

It wasn't long before Serge and Matt, who had been attending G4 though members at another church, asked Mateo about starting G4 at their church. This was a special time for everyone in G4. One of the large group times was set aside to commission Serge and Matt to launch a G4 ministry at their church. Everyone had a sense that they were living missionally, even as they were setting aside a season of their lives to overcome their own struggle.

Having two G4 ministries in the same community opened some excellent opportunities. First, new members to the addiction group could attend group more frequently in the early stages of pursuing sobriety. Second, the new church had a couple of groups that the first church did not have leaders for. This meant the new G4 ministry could serve their sending church in ways that it had originally served them.

Over the coming months, the ministry faced the perpetual challenges of a volunteer-based group: leaders would transition out, participants would relapse, occasionally a group would fold, and every now and again a crisis would arise. These things were sad, hard, and stressful. But the G4 ministry found its rhythm and had a growing reputation of trust in the church and community.

As the church tracked data compiling how people first heard about them, G4 served as a growing percentage of new members' first point of contact with the church. As more and more G4 graduates transitioned into the church's general small group ministry, they brought their level of transparency and desire for accountability with them. While their influence was hard to quantify, there was a palpable sense that small group prayer times were becoming more substantive and authentic.

The next year, as Pastor Philip set aside time to reflect on his time as pastor there, he considered G4. He called Trevor and Connor to see if they could go for breakfast. They went to the same greasy spoon restaurant that Trevor and Connor met at weekly just four years earlier. As they ate, they reflected on the unexpected journey that began with the statement, "If you come across any guys who need it, we'd be willing to start one of those G4 groups on Tuesday nights." It felt a bit surreal. Little had they known what God had in store from that simple offer of availability.

OBSERVATIONS ABOUT THIS STORY

I hope you found this story to be both motivating and realistic. I hope you say both "I *want* to do this" and "I think we *could actually* do this." As you reflect on this story, notice how G4 embodies the three core benefits of the lay-led ministry models this book strives to uphold.

1. *Compatibility with the local church*: G4 replicates like most church ministries. People get involved, benefit from and fall in love with the ministry, co-lead for a while, and then become the point leader for a new G4 group. As you will see more clearly in chapter 8, surprisingly few lay-based counseling models have been designed to harmonize with the naturally replicating ecosystem customary of most ministries in a local church.

2. *Sustainability*: G4 is designed to create a community of support among its leaders. Counseling is emotionally heavier than most ministries at your church. As G4 expands, the ministry design is highly intentional about creating a relational context that allows your leaders to thrive for years rather than burning out in months. Burnout amongst lay leaders in a counseling ministry is a leading reason church leaders sometimes think starting a counseling ministry was a mistake. Setting leaders up to thrive is essential for the long-term viability of your counseling ministry.

3. *Wisdom about issues of liability*: The primary way to reduce liability is truth in advertising (i.e., communicating clearly so that participants know what they're getting) and conducting a ministry as it's designed. G4 does not present itself as anything other than a lay-led ministry, and that fact, together with the familiarity many people have with groups like Alcoholics Anonymous and Celebrate Recovery means that new participants shouldn't come expecting the group facilitator to be a professional counselor.

Now that we've defined and illustrated G4, let's do the same for GCM.

Chapter 5

WHAT IS GCM?

We are moving from the more formal ministry of G4 to the less formal ministry of GCM. GCM mentoring is still more than friendship, but it does not require as much structure as G4. After GCM mentors are trained and paired with mentees, these relationships operate with significant freedom; while G4 groups meet on the same night of the week at the same location, GCM mentors and mentees meet whenever and wherever is best for them.

WHAT IS GCM?

Creating a Gospel-Centered Marriage (GCM) is a five-part series that serves as flexible curriculum for mentoring engaged couples and for marital enrichment within a church's small group ministry.[1] GCM provides marriage preparation and marriage enrichment content. (If a couple is in significant marital distress, they need marriage restoration-level care, which is more than GCM provides.)

In case you are unfamiliar with the categories of marriage preparation, marriage enrichment, and marriage restoration, here is a brief synopsis of each:

- *Marriage Preparation* helps engaged couples prepare for the new experience of marriage. It covers much of the same content that is covered in marriage enrichment material, but from

1. *Creating a Gospel-Centered Marriage* is available at www.bradhambrick.com/gcm.

the perspective of a couple looking ahead to marriage. GCM is designed to foster marriage preparation through mentoring relationships.

- *Marriage Enrichment* helps relatively healthy couples experience more fulfillment and joy in their marriages. Having couples with relatively healthy marriages work through marital maintenance material is the equivalent of someone who is relatively healthy joining the gym, improving their eating habits, and getting regular medical checkups. GCM is a marriage enrichment curriculum that couples can study in small groups (or under whatever name a church has for its primary discipleship groups).
- *Marriage Restoration* helps couples in crisis get to a healthy place. Marital crises might include infidelity, destructive communication patterns, or a spouse who is battling addiction. Restoration-level care requires the helper to have greater skill and training than GCM equips mentors or small group leaders to provide. However, GCM can serve as an aftercare resource once marriage restoration-level work has been adequately completed.

WHAT ARE THE GCM TOPICS?

The GCM curriculum is broken down into five major divisions, called seminars. The five seminars are Foundations, Communication, Finances, Decision-Making, and Intimacy. Each seminar is broken down into five or six smaller topics, each of which forms a lesson. The lessons are detailed here:

1. GCM: Foundations
- Lesson One: What Makes Marriage Hard?
- Lesson Two: What Makes Marriage Work?
- Lesson Three: Marriage as Covenant
- Lesson Four: Shared Marital Responsibilities of Husband and Wife
- Lesson Five: Unique Roles for the Husband
- Lesson Six: Unique Roles for the Wife

2. GCM: Communication
- Lesson One: What Makes Communication Hard?
- Lesson Two: Listening
- Lesson Three: Day-to-Day Communication
- Lesson Four: Conflict Resolution
- Lesson Five: Repentance
- Lesson Six: Forgiveness

3. GCM: Finances
- Lesson One: What Makes Finances Hard?
- Lesson Two: What Is a Budget?
- Lesson Three: A Budget You Can Manage in 30 Minutes Per Week
- Lesson Four: Getting Out of Debt
- Lesson Five: Getting into Savings

4. GCM: Decision-Making
- Lesson One: What Makes Decision-Making Hard?
- Lesson Two: Decision-Making and God's Will
- Lesson Three: Wise Practices for Individual Decision-Making
- Lesson Four: Wise Practices for Consensus Decision-Making
- Lesson Five: Wise Practices for Headship–Submission Decision-Making

5. GCM: Intimacy
- Lesson One: What Makes Romance Difficult?
- Lesson Two: Appreciating Our Differences
- Lesson Three: Living in the Larger Love Story of the Gospel
- Lesson Four: Sex as One of God's Gifts for Marriage (Part One)[2]
- Lesson Five: Sex as One of God's Gifts for Marriage (Part Two)

---

2. These later two units of the *GCM: Intimacy* seminar are not meant to be discussed in a small group setting. This material is best discussed between husband and wife.

As we explore the design of GCM, you will notice that although the lessons are the same for the marriage preparation mentorships as they are for the marriage enrichment small groups, they serve different functions in these two settings.

HOW DOES MENTORING FOR MARRIAGE PREPARATION WORK?

As we have seen, in GCM marriage preparation takes place in the context of mentoring relationships. Experienced married couples are trained to become mentors for couples who are planning to get married. The engaged couple walks through selections of the GCM material with the support and guidance of a more experienced couple.

It is recommended that mentor couples have been married for at least five years (your church may choose to increase this minimum) and are vetted by a pastor or GCM coordinator. This is to ensure that mentor couples represent a marriage your church desires to elevate in this type of ministry. Several questions to consider in this vetting process are provided in the launch plan found in chapter 16. Then selected mentors complete the training available at bradhambrick. com/gcm before they begin mentoring. (A mentor coordinator can also provide live renditions of this training, rather than relying on the GCM training video.)

Because the GCM mentor training gives a more thorough overview of the mentoring process and addresses the frequently asked questions of new mentors, the remainder of this chapter provides a CliffsNotes version of GCM to introduce you to this ministry.

The first meeting between mentors and mentees is focused on their getting to know one another. Lesson Two from *Creating a Gospel-Centered Marriage: Foundations* provides tools for mentors and mentees to share their stories and explore their personalities to facilitate getting to know each other.

After that, the next five meetings follow the same basic process. That process includes the following:

- The engaged couple completes an evaluation before meeting with the mentor couple.

- Based on these results, the mentor couple chooses the best-fitting lesson or lessons from the next GCM seminar.
- Mentors and mentees study the chosen lesson(s) to discuss at their next meeting.
- When they meet, the couples discuss the questions at the end of each lesson.

Drawing material from select lesson(s) of the five broader seminars helps to ensure that the premarital preparation for every engaged couple is holistic. Yet this process is also tailored: each couple is guided to the content from each GCM section that best fits their relational needs. This approach also means that mentors engage with different marital enrichment content each time they go through the process.

The role of the mentor couple is to draw from their life experience to illustrate and give testimony to the principles in the GCM series. Mentoring relationships should be a welcoming place for the engaged couples to ask questions. Having a trusted, experienced couple to talk with during their engagement and the early years of marriage usually exceeds the benefit of the educational content in the GCM series. Although the formal mentoring meetings end with the wedding, the relationship between mentors and mentees does not; instead, it is transformed into an ongoing friendship.

WHY MENTORING?

The most common form of premarital preparation in Christian circles is three to six formal pastoral counseling sessions. This model is different. Why? The answer doesn't have to do with the *content* of the counsel received. The content is essentially the same in both approaches.

The advantage of GCM is the *relational dynamics* that differ between pastoral counseling and mentoring. When a couple does their premarital work via pastoral counseling, what does it look like for them to reach out for help during the inevitable ups and downs of their first year of marriage? They must call the church to make an appointment with the pastor—a daunting task. A newly married couple is unlikely to do that until things are "that bad." That means the call for help is unlikely to be in the early stages of difficulty, when the challenge is easiest to resolve and has done the least amount of damage.

Mentoring changes this dynamic. Meeting with a married couple in their home, sharing meals together as they talk, and experiencing a relationship of learning alongside one another makes it easier for the newlywed couple to reach out when they need help later. They're not making an appointment, but calling experienced friends.

This is the big win of GCM mentoring. After all, as most married people can admit, it was hard to understand the significance of everything we learned about marriage during premarital counseling. Even if the education was excellent, the retention was lacking—while we planned a wedding and only guessed what marriage would be like. Having follow-up conversations with mentors to review and apply what we learned would have been much more effective.

WHAT ABOUT MARRIAGE ENRICHMENT STUDIES WITHIN SMALL GROUPS?

The same GCM curriculum that is used in premarital mentoring can also be used for marriage enrichment—but the relationship in which it is utilized changes. Unlike GCM used for premarital mentoring, a GCM seminar studied in a small group is part of the church's existing discipleship ministry.

While the GCM material includes topics often talked about in a counseling setting, when these materials are worked through in a naturally paired environment—like a small group—that doesn't involve the disclosure of privileged information; it is not "counseling." Instead, it is a discussion among friends for their mutual edification. GCM for marriage enrichment is thus part of the ongoing building up of one another that happens within the church.

Let me explain. If you think *counseling* simply means being helpful (as if everything helpful was inherently counseling), then it doesn't make sense to say GCM in one setting is counseling and in another setting is discipleship. As you will see in section two, calling something counseling means that there are clear helper–helpee roles that result in the disclosure of privileged information. Seeing this difference will help your church differentiate counseling from general discipleship (including GCM) and thereby rightly honor the information shared in a counseling context.

As has been mentioned, each GCM seminar is broken down into five or six lessons. This means that each seminar can be its own five- or six-week study. The content exists in three forms: written materials, video teaching, and audio podcast. Each small group member can choose which form best fits their learning style and schedule. In addition, there are discussion questions with each lesson. If the group chooses to use the videos, they can use the first fifteen minutes of their time to watch a video together as a precursor to engaging the discussion questions.

Each lesson has exercises, discussion prompts, or tools that individual couples can use to enrich their marriage. These are activities that couples are more likely to do together outside of the small group discussion. In effect, these exercises serve as marriage enrichment homework for the small group study.

WHAT ABOUT POSTMARITAL MENTORING?

In general, GCM is used in mentorships for marriage preparation and in small groups for marriage enrichment. However, churches frequently ask whether they can use GCM as a postmarital mentoring resource. Yes, if you can ensure that what the couple needs is truly marriage enrichment and not marriage restoration. If a church attempts to use GCM to help a mentee couple that has marriage restoration-level needs, two undesirable things will result.

First, that church is not going to serve the mentee couple well. Marriage enrichment advice for marriage restoration-level problems is like telling someone about the exercise routine they should have used to avoid the heart attack they are currently experiencing. The exercise routine may be excellent, but it is not what is needed at that moment.

Second, you are going to see a high burnout rate in your mentor population. Mentoring removes the social barriers that exist with more formal forms of counseling. Mentoring happens at kitchen tables and in living rooms. When you ask lay mentors to regularly invite crisis-level care into their homes, it is going to emotionally deplete them to a degree that they may no longer have the bandwidth to serve in your ministry. Understanding this is essential to having a relationally sustainable ministry for your volunteers.

This matter reinforces one of the foundational principles of this book: *know the limits of what your counseling ministry can do well*. When a couple's need goes beyond your counseling ministry's capacity to care well—that is, beyond the care that mentors facilitating a curriculum can give—realize that doesn't mean your church is unwilling to be involved. It means that supportive friendships and pastoral care are what your church has to offer as you encourage the couple to seek a counselor with the training to help them navigate their marital crisis.

ACCEPTING GCM'S LIMITATIONS

Talking about the limits of GCM is not an exciting crescendo for this chapter. But my goal isn't primarily to motivate you; it's to equip you to lead a counseling ministry. With that in mind, it is important for you, as the leader of this ministry, to maintain your enthusiasm without becoming discouraged by what the ministry doesn't do.

Imagine this difficult conversation: a couple is separated because one partner is having an emotional affair and requests a GCM mentor. You explain with compassion that GCM is not designed for what they are facing. You pray with them, recommend a quality marriage counselor, and connect them with a pastor for pastoral care.

Although this couple may be dissatisfied, you don't need to feel guilty that you didn't force a lay mentor into a role they were ill-equipped to take on. Acknowledging the limitations of your church's ministry doesn't need to dampen the satisfaction you take from the premarital couples being blessed or the marriage enrichment happening in small groups. It is essential for the leader of a church-based counseling ministry not to allow compassion for needs the ministry is not equipped to meet to rob them of the satisfaction that comes from the good things the ministry is doing.

Chapter 6

A GRASSROOTS LAUNCH STORY
FOR GCM

We are going to stick with the premise that in most churches, most new ministries launch without a major initiative or a paid staff person to oversee them. Ministries that must start big tend to only start at big churches. It shouldn't be the case that counseling ministries are only viable for big churches.

Just as we did with G4, we'll tell a story about the launch and growth of GCM. Remember, this story is just one example of how things *might* start; read it like a testimonial, not a procedural manual. (That will be coming in chapter 16).

THE STORY BEGINS

Jason and Lisa were nearing retirement, but not slowing down. Over the years, they had gotten to know most every ministry of the church as their two children grew up. In recent years, both of their children went away to college, got engaged, and got married. As a result, Jason and Lisa heard how two different churches handled premarital counseling. Hearing what their son, daughter-in-law, daughter, and son-in-law thought about their premarital experiences sparked Jason and Lisa to ask what this looks like at their church. What *could* it look like?

When they asked Pastor Brian these questions, he told them he meets with each couple three to four times, gives them his favorite book on marriage, and recommends a local counselor for additional care, if desired. Lisa couldn't help but ask, "Would you mind if we looked into how we might start a premarital ministry at our church?" Pastor Brian was happy to set them free on this expedition.

After looking at various books and ministry models, Jason and Lisa settled on the *Creating a Gospel-Centered Marriage* (GCM) mentoring series. They liked that it involved older couples in the church as mentors, that evaluations tailored the mentoring experience to each engaged couple, and that there was a video teaching component so that mentors didn't feel pressured to be marriage experts. Pastor Brian liked that the program was biblically based, had a redemptive tone, and was developed in a church for church-based implementation.

Jason and Lisa went through the free mentor training at bradhambrick.com/gcm. After that, although they were a little nervous, they felt ready to learn alongside the first couple they could mentor. Dalton and Ginger had recently gotten engaged and asked Pastor Brian to officiate their wedding. When he asked if they'd like to do premarital counseling by mentoring, they loved the idea. Looking back, Pastor Brian says, "I think that's when we launched our premarital mentoring ministry."

Over the next six months, Jason and Lisa met with Dalton and Ginger. Things seemed pretty simple. The first meeting was spent getting to know each other using two resources from the GCM series. After that, Dalton and Ginger completed an evaluation of their relationship to determine which lesson from the next GCM seminar to study and discuss with Jason and Lisa.

Most of their meetings were at Jason and Lisa's home, although they held one meeting over dinner at a restaurant. Conversations were relaxed, but structured, as they used the GCM discussion questions. They always chased a few rabbits as Jason and Lisa shared stories about the early years of their marriage and a few lessons they learned the hard way. These stories helped Dalton and Ginger relax enough to ask more authentic questions regarding fears or uncertainties about marriage. Even with this greater vulnerability, they laughed a lot and developed a deep friendship.

Jason and Lisa were struck by how meaningful it was to attend Dalton and Ginger's wedding. When they received Dalton and Ginger's first Christmas card, they read the enclosed letter like it was from one of their children. It was almost as exciting to get the "we're expecting" announcement from Dalton and Ginger as it was from their own children. Jason and Lisa realized GCM was a way for them to impact generations in other families.

Their excitement made recruiting new mentors easy. They talked about Dalton and Ginger in their small group like they talked about their own children. Lisa did the same at her women's Bible study, as did Jason at the men's gathering. Jason and Lisa didn't recruit. They just talked about something they enjoyed.

Soon, ten couples wanted to be mentors. Jason and Lisa agreed to serve as the mentor coordinators when Pastor Brian connected the newly engaged couples with them. Now they had a different problem: the supply of mentors exceeded the demand of engaged couples in the church. Although Pastor Brian made mentoring the standard premarital approach for the church, they still had more mentors than mentees. This highlighted that college and young professional aged members were a smaller part of the church's demographic.

The church took a two-pronged approach to finding more engaged couples. First, they reached out to Dalton and Ginger and the other couples who had been mentored. Dalton and Ginger had already talked to their friends about how much Jason and Lisa meant to them. But they didn't realize that they could suggest this kind of mentoring relationship as an opportunity for their friends who were getting engaged.

Second, they contacted the campus ministries at the local colleges, both the university and the junior college. The church had long wanted a better relationship with these schools. GCM gave them something to offer the college ministries to forge a partnership. A steady stream of engaged couples emerged.

This relationship between the church and the college ministry benefited many students who were graduating. Many college students were treating the college ministry as if it was their church. The local college ministry staff observed that many students had no church home after graduating. For engaged students, GCM made finding a church family easy. Also, many of the non-engaged graduates who stayed in town got connected with the church through their friends.

An unexpected blessing emerged from engaged friends of GCM graduates. Several of these couples were both unchurched and not Christians. When Dalton and Ginger saw two of their friends come to faith as they were mentored, it generated a new level of excitement for GCM.

GCM strengthened the church in two unexpected ways. First, the church began to see their college and young professional age group grow. That wasn't why they started GCM; it was just a side effect. Second, an intergenerational connection emerged through each mentoring relationship. Everyone in the church began to note that GCM was a catalyst for the church to feel more and more like a family.

The growing reputation of GCM in the church generated new questions. Mentor couples wanted relationships that would help their marriages the way the mentoring relationships had helped newly married couples. They bumped their heads against the idea that, at a certain age, they wouldn't be able to have *older* couples mentor them, and yet even tenured marriages benefit from the sharpening of intentional relationships with other couples.

It was Deion and Aliyah who realized that each GCM seminar also works as a small group study. It made sense that small groups were a natural place for experienced couples to gain the benefits of intentional relationships with other experienced married couples. In small group leader meetings, Pastor Brian mentioned a GCM seminar as an option for groups with married couples. The number of small groups with a GCM mentor couple already attending meant that groups were excited to do a GCM study annually.

This had the following two effects: First, it created a culture of marriage enrichment among the experienced couples in the church.

Periodically doing a GCM study meant that there didn't have to be a reason to ask each other how their marriage was doing. It became easier—even expected—for every couple to acknowledge areas where they needed to grow. Second, because of the growing marriage enrichment culture, it became clear that some marriages that had been moderately struggling began to thrive. For these marriages, the support of friends and the principles of GCM made a world of difference. What they needed was a prompt to stop ignoring the problem and a context of accountability for making basic changes to improve their relationships.

Other couples, however, were in greater distress. Jason and Lisa, as the most experienced mentors at church, tried mentoring Eric and Bethany and found that mentoring a couple in high distress was quite different from other mentoring relationships. Eric and Bethany would try to get Jason and Lisa to take sides in their arguments, and Eric and Bethany had different versions of what caused the problems. Jason and Lisa weren't sure how to adjudicate the differences (or even if that was their role).

The information they were getting was weighty. Confidentiality meant Jason and Lisa had to carry it alone. Also, Jason and Lisa couldn't schedule meetings with Eric and Bethany at a restaurant or when their children were at home. The social dynamics made many settings off limits.

Further, Eric and Bethany often felt like the GCM curriculum provided only a Band-Aid solution for their more intense marital difficulties. Meanwhile, Jason and Lisa felt like they were failing.

In a conversation with Pastor Brian about the challenges of postmarital mentoring, it was decided that GCM was not a good fit for marriages in high distress. They began to see how marriage preparation and marriage enrichment work differed from marriage restoration work. As they prayed about what to do, Raudel and Sophia mentioned to Pastor Brian their burden for high distress marriages.

With Pastor Brian's blessing, Raudel and Sophia started a G4 ministry. Initially, they began an anger group because anger was the primary disrupter of effective mentoring in high distress marriages. Raudel led a group for men, while Sophia led a group for women. Because they wanted these groups to be marriage focused, they grew accustomed to saying, "We know anger may not be the biggest problem in your marriage, but learning to manage your anger is likely the first skill toward restoring your marriage." Eventually, *False Love* and *True Betrayal* groups were also started, as infidelity, pornography, and betrayal arose as prevalent themes. Even with these groups in place, they still needed to recommend good marriage counselors. Often the G4 groups served as peer support for each spouse while they attended marriage counseling together.

As the church figured out how to care for people in high distress marriages, the rest of GCM continued to flourish. Periodically, common problems would emerge. For example, an engaged couple would be living together,[1] a marriage had abusive dynamics, or one partner was struggling with addiction. It was hard when mentors couldn't affirm a couple's desire to get married or had to ask a couple to tell their pastor they were living together. But Jason and Lisa got comfortable with their role as GCM mentor coordinators, which included encouraging mentors who were navigating these unpleasant parts of mentoring.

Jason and Lisa realized that their database of mentors and mentees provided the opportunity to raise awareness for marriage conferences in their area. Usually, they had enough interest to get a group discount rate for attendees from their church. While couples would travel to the event separately, they would often schedule a group dinner before or after the conference to build fellowship among the couples from their church. These conference times continued to build on the emerging marriage enrichment culture at their church and exposed couples to fresh voices talking about marriage.

The GCM ministry began to host an annual mentor–mentee dinner around Valentine's Day. It was a time to celebrate all that God had done through this ministry. Tenured mentoring couples like

---

1. For guidance on how this conversation might be handled, consider "Cohabitation: A Conversation Starter," bradhambrick.com/cohabitation.

Jason and Lisa had to gather multiple tables to fit in their large GCM family tree.

As Pastor Brian prepared his remarks to celebrate the seventh anniversary of GCM in the church, he realized that the mentoring ministry had affected their church in ways that far exceeded marriage enrichment. With reflection, he saw growth in the college and young professionals segments of their church, a church culture that encouraged people to take initiative in starting new ministries, and a tangible growth in the intergenerational relationships within the church. The theme of his talk was: "The nonmarital reasons I enjoy pastoring this church more because of GCM."

OBSERVATIONS ABOUT THIS STORY

I hope you found this story to be both motivating and realistic. GCM may be one of the most rewarding and enriching ministries you can launch at your church. Experienced couples investing in the lives of engaged couples produce some of the sweetest and most lasting relationships in a church—relationships that will bless family trees for generations to come.

As you think over this story, you should notice the following familiar features with GCM that were also noted with G4:

Church compatible: GCM mentoring is designed so that these volunteers still have the capacity to lead in other ministries of the church. While most counseling-related ministries are emotionally weighty enough that they comprise a volunteer's exclusive ministry role, getting dinner with an engaged couple every three to four weeks and learning alongside them isn't overwhelming. And using GCM as a small group study promotes marriage enrichment within the church without adding anything new to the church calendar. The weekly meeting rhythm of small groups provides support and encouragement for these marriages.

Relationally sustainable: Recognizing the difference in emotional weight between premarital mentoring and marriage enrichment as compared to caring for couples in need of restoration-level care helps ensure that GCM leaders don't burn out by regularly adding crises to their lives.

Liability wise: GCM as a small group study doesn't involve disclosing privileged information (we'll define that more in chapters 9 and 13). Everything is discussed in an open environment of mutual support. GCM as premarital mentoring creates the freedom to talk about public excitement over the coming wedding without going into personal details. It's a ministry that naturally builds its own enthusiasm without creating contexts prone to confidentiality violations.

In these first six chapters we've cultivated enthusiasm for the lives that will be changed through G4 and GCM. Now we begin the hard work of creating the context that allows this change to happen.

Section One:
Navigating Common Points
of Confusion

As you are beginning to launch a counseling ministry consisting of groups (G4) and mentoring relationships (GCM), many people, maybe including you, will have questions like these: Why are we doing it this way? What challenges are we avoiding with this less formal approach? What options are we foregoing? How do we explain the advantages of this approach to church members who expected something more like professional counseling? We will answer these kinds of questions in section one.

Chapter 7

PARABLE OF THE DARK ROOM:
THE FEAR OF LIABILITY

We have agreed that a counseling ministry is a good thing. But even a wisely developed counseling ministry exposes a church to various types of liability in ways that other ministries do not. Liability concerns are often misunderstood by churches. Too often, we only think about not getting sued, but that is a low bar of ethical consideration about liability. Yes, liability involves the possibility of a lawsuit, but if managed poorly, a counseling ministry can cost your church its reputation in the community, trust of members, and unity within the body. These things are harder to recoup than money.

A counseling ministry will invite people to be vulnerable about the most sensitive areas of their lives. As you think about how to structure a counseling ministry, you are preparing to honor and steward this information well. Two primary issues that create liability are mishandling this information or misrepresenting the qualifications of your counselors. They can cost your church money, reputation, trust, and unity. In the chapters ahead, you will learn how to avoid both missteps.

With that in mind, you are ready for a modern parable that captures the experience of many—perhaps most—church leaders as they consider the possibility of starting a counseling ministry.

PARABLE

A married couple explores a house they want to buy. They walk into the kitchen, and they know what to look for: type of stove (gas or electric), floor plan (open-island concept or closed off), and general decor. The same is true in the living room, master bedroom, and bathrooms. (Can you tell my wife likes HGTV?)

But then they come to a room I'll call the sitting room. Most homes don't have one of these. There are no windows to let light in. By the light filtering in from the hallway, they can tell the room is crowded with furniture. In the middle of the room there is an elegant (i.e., expensive) vase on a pillar stand (i.e., not the most stable of tables). Instead of stepping into this room, the couple gets nervous and decides to go check out the guest bedroom.

INTERPRETATION

Churches consider new ministry initiatives the way this couple explored the house they wanted to buy. The rooms in this parable represent different areas of ministry. When ministry leaders look to expand the ministry offerings of their church, they usually know the predominant models for each area: worship (hymns or contemporary), small groups (missional communities or Sunday school), student ministry (youth group or whole-family based), etc.

But then someone says, "We should start a *counseling ministry* at our church." No one disagrees, but the idea's like that dark sitting room. Not many churches have a counseling ministry, so it's unknown territory. The furniture represents the various rules and regulations associated with counseling. The dim light represents the limited understanding ministry leaders have of these things. The expensive vase in the middle of the room represents liability. After a bit of conversation while standing in the doorway looking in, the church leaders get nervous and decide to start a local outreach initiative instead.

IMPLICATIONS

The reality is we have an uphill journey to launch counseling ministries. *Liability concerns are not fake fears.* The vase is real and really expensive (not just monetarily) if knocked over.

A counseling ministry is tricky because counselors are entrusted with people's personal information, which is privileged when shared within a counseling relationship. Inappropriate sharing of such information is not just *gossip* (a moral term); it is a *breach of confidentiality* (a legal term). In some cases, that information may live forever on paper known as case notes (which we'll talk more about in chapter 13).

While in most other areas, a church being transparent with documents is seen as a virtue, in a counseling ministry, disclosure of a counselee's information should happen only with their permission. Who should see the case notes, when, and under what conditions? Can the senior pastor or elders see them because of their roles? For reasons that will be explored in future chapters, the answer is no— not without the individual's permission.

A counseling ministry is also tricky to promote. It's essential to give people accurate information, but doing so can be verbally cumbersome. Think about the way churches promote ministries. Generally, a Sunday morning announcement is adequate informed consent: "Come be a part of our Wednesday night Bible study on the Psalms." But when it comes to talking about a counseling ministry, mentioning the details that entail an accurate portrayal of what the ministry is and isn't can feel like the equivalent of an FDA warning label on a prescription.

When promoting our church's ministries, we're used to celebrating everything we do with superlatives. Clarifying the things our counseling ministry does and doesn't do, the training the ministry leaders do and don't have, and explaining a counselee's right to discontinue counseling anytime they choose feels awkward for a church ministry announcement.

Lack of understanding of the possible models for church-based counseling ministries creates another obstacle. I remember when I interviewed for my current role as pastor of counseling. Most of the questions were what I call "jellyfish questions" (lacking structure), and I had to provide the skeleton (key concepts and options). Here's what that conversation looked like:

Question: If we hired you, how would you recommend we provide counsel for those who are depressed at our church?

My Answer: That depends on who is giving the care and what role they are in. Are we talking about (a) someone caring for a friend in small group; (b) a support group for depression; (c) someone serving as a lay counselor; or (d) connecting someone with a professional in our community? Each of these roles requires a different type of training and has different rules.

Their Response: Is one approach more biblical or effective than the others? If not, when would we do each? This is where we get confused. Counseling feels like it plays by its own rules that no one ever explains.

My Answer: Let me tell you about the early draft of my book. I was, and still am, learning how to best differentiate these things.

Most decision-makers in churches inadequately understand the differences in various counseling ministry options that can exist in a local church. After all, can you define the pertinent differences (roles, guidelines, training level, etc.) in these four approaches?

1. Friendship or care via a small group
2. Peer-led counseling groups or mentoring relationships
3. Lay counseling with intake forms and case notes
4. Professional counseling

Looking at the list above, you probably have an intuitive sense that there are differences and that these differences are important, but you may have a hard time putting those differences into words. Are you getting the feeling that you're looking into the dark room?

When important distinctions are not clear, we tend to want to make bold assertions ("every helpful conversation is counseling" or "only professionals should do counseling") that oversimplify what confuses us. Do you feel the fear of that dark room with the expensive vase?

Did you notice something might be missing from the list? As someone wanting to start a church-based counseling ministry, you may look at this list and ask, "Where is the pastor? Is counseling with a pastor the same as one or more of these situations, or is it different from all of them?" Good question. We'll speak to that in chapter 10. For now, we're simply clarifying the confusion that exists among these options.

These are difficult waters to navigate, and a church that wants to set up some form of counseling ministry needs to understand clearly what models exist and what the advantages and disadvantages of each model are—including the liability the church may incur with a particular model.

Although these are complicated matters, you can probably tell that my goal in this book is to write in common language and illustrations as much as possible. We will discuss technical concepts, such as confidentiality, formality, and jurisdiction, and as we do so, I will strive to honor the importance of these subjects. But my goal is to discuss them in the common language of a church foyer because that is where the implications will have to be explained and lived out.

NAVIGATING VASE PHOBIA

I want to clarify something to help with our vase phobia. *The ethical mistakes churches make in counseling aren't usually a result of asking the right questions and choosing unethical answers. We make ethical mistakes because we don't know the right question we should have asked (past tense) until it's too late.*

For example, we often miss when the nature of a relationship changes, so we don't recognize when the rules for care change. A conversation starts casually, but then it begins to get weighty and the information disclosed becomes personal. When does the conversation become counseling? Is it the setting that matters (church foyer, coffee shop, private office)? Is it the weight of what is being shared (it's counseling only if the helpee cries)? Is it the training or role of the person listening?

These considerations raise a point we will elaborate on later. *When we call a ministry "counseling," we are implying that the helper in the relationship knows the correct answers to these questions and can guide the relationship accordingly.* It is not the helpee's responsibility to know the answers to these questions when they reach out for help. For a church-based counseling ministry, this also means that church leadership needs to understand these guidelines well enough to honor your emerging counseling ministry. That's why you are encouraged to review this book with your pastoral leadership before taking steps to implement what you're learning.

This doesn't have to be scary; it should be humbling. When things are set up well and managed properly, these questions don't have to make us feel we're in a maze. But we should also realize that *a sincere desire to help is not all that is needed to effectively start a counseling ministry.*

FROM LIABILITY TO SUSTAINABILITY

In this chapter, we illustrated the first fear many churches have about starting a counseling ministry—liability. This is a concern that most church leaders can put into words. In the next chapter, we'll put into words a concern that is harder for many churches to articulate but is an equal deterrent to a church's willingness to start a counseling ministry.

Chapter 8

THE CHALLENGE OF SUSTAINABILITY: HR STEWARDSHIP AND BURNOUT

As we begin this chapter, let's use our imaginations again, this time to delve into the concern of *sustainability*. A counseling ministry can be administratively and emotionally overwhelming if we're unaware of the challenges. So as you begin your ministry, you'll want to understand the potential challenges and design the emerging ministry in a way that accounts for them.

STARTING A COUNSELING MINISTRY: A PSEUDO-PROFESSIONAL APPROACH

Most often, when churches imagine starting a counseling ministry, they envision a pseudo-professional model in which members of their church go through some type of training and begin meeting with members of the congregation and community. These meetings happen by appointment and involve intake forms and case notes that must be stored and managed.

Imagine what the process of launching this type of ministry entails. First, a church is going to select its most mature and capable lay leaders. We intuitively realize that this type of counseling ministry is too weighty to be led by those lacking maturity or the capacity to navigate emotionally and relationally intense situations. This means that starting a counseling ministry requires a church to devote its best leaders to this task.

However, leadership will soon realize that maturity alone does not equip someone to be a lay counselor—at least to the level of promoting what these individuals do as "counseling" on the church website and pairing them with strangers seeking help for acute life challenges. Therefore, to start a counseling ministry, a church must ask its best leaders to commit to a season of training. Depending on the training organization chosen, most lay counseling training usually takes twelve to eighteen months for completion.

At the end of that training, these leaders probably have a capacity to take on two to four counseling cases at one time. If these individuals work full time or have family responsibilities (which most will), then taking on more than two to four cases would put them on a quick path to burnout.

But it gets worse. These two to four cases typically have an extended duration. It is rare for a hardship that merits counseling to be resolved in a few weekly meetings. This means that these best leaders of your church will take on two to four cases, most of which will last for multiple months.

There's more. Traditional counselees don't graduate from being counseled into serving as counselors. Churches are used to ministries that replicate from within. For example, someone joins a small group, learns what the church desires small groups to do, becomes a co-leader of the group, and then launches their own small group as the group grows. Almost every church-based ministry operates in this kind of ecosystem. But a pseudo-professional counseling ministry doesn't. That means every new lay counselor—whether required by attrition of existing lay counselors or the demand for more counseling—must start at the beginning of this journey.

Whether a given church can articulate these difficulties or not, there is an intuitive sense that these challenges exist, and it makes the aspiration of starting a counseling ministry seem unachievable. G4 and GCM were designed to account for these challenges.

Important point: *The church cannot privatize discipleship.* Whatever we aspire to do when creating a counseling ministry, we cannot create a system within which every person gets their own private counselor. This would be unsustainable and would not be faithful to God's design for the church. Moreover, most of the care within a church will always be conveyed not through programs but through friendships.[1] When a church creates a counseling ministry, it should be a ministry in which people receive help for a season and then transition back into the church's regular discipleship ministries. A counseling ministry is auxiliary to the ongoing discipleship ministries of the church.

Further, a church's capacity to provide lay counseling is necessarily limited by the experience, passion, and willingness of those available to lead. You may want to start groups to address addiction, but for this to be viable, you will need a leader with experience overcoming addiction. The human resources of the church will determine which needs it can effectively address.

What all of that means: *To be sustainable, a church's counseling ministry must be compatible with how that church functions.* As we just illustrated, the pseudo-professional model of lay counseling doesn't match the way training and replication typically happen in church life. Only the pastoral staff complete a level of training comparable to what we described. To expect an elaborate training process for a lay ministry is not viable for most churches.

For a counseling ministry to be sustainable, it needs to have a shorter training process, allow people to utilize their life experiences as part of their qualifications, and have a leadership development plan that allows participants to mature into new leaders via their participation in the ministry. Again, that is the design of G4 and GCM.

---

1. Friendship ministry is not something a church launches, but it is something a church can and should intentionally enrich. My forthcoming book in this series, *Transformative Friendships: 7 Questions to Deepen Any Relationship* (Greensboro, NC: New Growth Press, 2024), equips your church to cultivate a culture of deep and caring friendships within the congregation.

STARTING A COUNSELING MINISTRY: A GROUPS AND MENTORING APPROACH

Let's reenvision what a counseling ministry might look like, using a groups and mentoring approach instead of a pseudo-professional approach. This description will reinforce many of the principles you saw illustrated in the stories of G4 and GCM in chapters 4 and 6.

In this version, counselors are more facilitators than experts. In this model, lay leaders use their life experience paired with a relevant curriculum to care for people with a shared life experience. The structure of the ministry positions the helper as more than just a friend, but without the expectations of being pseudo-professional.

Because the leaders are not being asked to be general practitioners of counseling, the duration of their training can be brief. They need to know how to lead a group or be a mentor[2] and be familiar with the curriculum that guides the counseling process for the particular subject they will be addressing. Most of their training happened as they overcame their life struggle (in the case of G4 leaders) or navigated the major life transition of getting married (in the case of GCM mentors).

Furthermore, the G4 and GCM curriculums guard against leaders getting in over their heads by including assessments for participants to use to identify higher-level concerns than G4 or GCM are designed to address. When higher-level concerns exist, the curriculum recommends that the participant seek more professional care. These embedded assessments and recommendations remove the necessity of the lay leader having to introduce an awkward conversation about seeking additional care. The curriculum initiates these conversations for them.

The G4 and GCM models also guard the leaders' time. Unlike friends, these lay leaders do not just hang out with anyone who is hurting whenever it's needed. The church is not assigning therapeutic friends to hurting members, which would be a recipe for burnout. If

---

2. *Facilitating Counseling Groups* gives G4 group leaders the guidance they need, and the online GCM *Mentor Training Manual* (with its accompanying video) provides guidance for GCM mentors.

friendship could provide adequate resolution for someone's struggle, that individual would be pointed toward the church's small group or discipleship ministry.

Each lay leader has just one area of care (addiction, depression, premarital mentoring, etc.), and there is defined process for connecting participants with that care. Having a designated setting for care and a defined method of connection makes the ministry more emotionally and relationally sustainable for these lay leaders.

It also means that these lay leaders don't respond to requests like, "Would you go talk to my uncle? He's an alcoholic but doesn't want to admit it. Here's his number. Will you call him?" or "My son wants to get married, but I think his fiancée is cheating on him. Would one of your mentors reach out to him?" Instead, people are welcome to *come to* G4 and GCM, but the counseling ministry does not *go to* those who do not voluntarily seek care.

In addition, group leaders and mentors have peers who are serving as they are serving. Once several groups or a mentoring program gets started, the leaders within these ministries begin to provide encouragement for one another. This means that leaders don't feel like serving in the counseling ministry puts them on a relational island.

Another advantage of the G4/GCM model over the pseudo-professional model is that it solves the problem of raising up new leaders. In group ministry, as some members mature, they can begin to take on the role of co-leader. As the group grows, a co-leader can launch a new group so that the size of the group remains optimal for the growth of its members.

Finally, G4 ministry design gives its leaders the ability to help more people at one time. Whereas a pseudo-professional lay counselor can be reasonably expected to work with only two to four people at a time, a G4 leader can serve six to twelve people at one time because of the group format and the mutual support that emerges between members of the group. And GCM mentors, because of their narrowly defined role, maintain the capacity to serve in other ministries within the church while being GCM leaders.

Doubtless you have a dozen "how" questions popping into your mind. That's good. It means you have seen how groups and mentoring allow a counseling ministry to fit naturally into your local church—and that has made you excited about the possibilities ahead. We'll lay a little more foundation, and then in Section Three we'll discuss how you can start making these possibilities a reality.

Chapter 9

STAYING IN OUR CHOSEN LANE:
WHAT IS COUNSELING?

Type B people are going to love this chapter. Type A people, well, I think you'll enjoy this chapter once you accept that we won't be able to provide as many details as you desire.

Counseling is a word like *dog*. It has a broad semantic range. *Dog* can mean everything from Toy Poodle (a cat that barks) to Great Dane (a horse that people allow to live in their house). Similarly, counseling can mean everything from "every helpful conversation" to "a professional relationship with a credentialed helper."

My purpose in this chapter is not to say which definition is correct. There are many legitimate uses of the term *counseling*. Instead, I want to make sure that a church is *clear* about what it means when referencing its counseling ministry. Clarity is the first essential part of doing counseling well in the local church. Consider the following statements that might be heard in church:

- "After services we will have pastors and prayer *counselors* available for anyone who feels led to respond to today's sermon."
- "We are excited about the ways people in our church's small groups *counsel* one another through hard times and difficult decisions."

- "Our church has support groups for addictions, grief, and other life struggles for those who would like *counseling* for these struggles."
- "Our church has a lay *counseling* ministry in case you are facing a set of life challenges that you're not yet comfortable sharing with your small group."
- "If you would like a recommendation for a licensed *counselor* in our community who will honor your Christian values, we are happy to make a recommendation."

Are these five uses of the term *counsel, counselor*, or *counseling* the same? No, and the differences are important. Are these five uses of the term *counsel, counselor*, or *counseling* legitimate? Yes, but a church would be using definitional sleight of hand if they used these meanings interchangeably.

So, what is **the main point of this chapter**? *When a church uses the term counseling, we must be clear about the type of care we are providing*. In the context of professional counseling, this is called informed consent, meaning the person receiving care is given the information necessary to consent to the type of care they are receiving. In ministry-based care, this clarity is still essential.

To help you provide this clarity, we will examine five ways your church might use the word *counseling*. They are arranged from the least to most formal. Your church already has a level-one counseling ministry and likely refers people to level four and five resources in your community. The ministries we are focusing on—G4 and GCM—are level-two counseling ministries.

FIVE LEVELS OF COMPETENCE IN COUNSELING[1]

"Levels of competence" are not defined by Scripture. Like pastor-to-member ratios, the frequency with which a church takes the

---

1. This material is a substantially revised version of "The Competency of the Biblical Counselor," the chapter I contributed to *Scripture and Counseling: God's Word for Life in a Broken World* edited by Bob Kellemen and Jeff Forrey (Grand Rapids: Zondervan, 2014). The original chapter was written for a general audience. This rendition has been narrowed to focus on implementing G4 and GCM ministries.

Lord's Supper, the training needed to become a pastor, and worship styles, the Bible leaves it open for individual churches to decide what level of counseling care they are able to offer their congregations.

In this book, you are being equipped to start a level-two counseling ministry. Understanding how this type of ministry compares with other possible models will equip you to communicate clearly with church leadership, your congregation, and those receiving care.

The five levels of counseling competence we will discuss are . . .

1. one-another ministry;
2. peer support and mentoring;
3. educated counselors;
4. experienced counselors; and
5. counseling specialists.

All these levels might be found in a church or other Christian setting. It is helpful to also know the secular vocational equivalents of these five types of counseling.

Categories for this Chapter	Secular, Professional Equivalents
One-Another Ministry	N/A—this is friends and family
Peer Support and Mentoring	Alcoholics Anonymous, Other 12-Step Groups, the National Alliance on Mental Illness (NAMI), etc.
Educated Counselors	Licensed Counselor at the Associate Level: LMHCA, LPCA, LMFTA, LCSWA
Experienced Counselors	LMHC, LPC, LMFT, LCSW
Counseling Specialists	Counseling Specialists, Residential Counseling

It is also helpful to know the forms these five types of counseling often take in a church or other Christian setting.

Categories for this Chapter	Church-Related Expressions
One-Another Ministry	People in the same small group or ministry team
Peer Support and Mentoring	G4, GCM, *Celebrate Recovery, Divorce Care, Grief Share*
Educated Counselors	Counseling models utilizing certified lay counselors
Experienced Counselors	Professional parachurch counseling centers
Counseling Specialists	Christian-based residential programs

In order to help you compare and contrast these types of counseling, we will now examine each one using the same five categories: (1) scope of ministry; (2) level of training; (3) level of experience; (4) advantages and opportunities; and (5) limitations and weaknesses.

LEVEL ONE: ONE-ANOTHER MINISTRY

Every church already has this type of counseling ministry. This is the level at which we all offer counseling every day. We listen to our friends share about their struggles, make some evaluation, and offer words of encouragement or guidance. However, for the purposes of this book, I recommend using the term *care* instead of *counseling* to describe one-another ministry.

Scope of Ministry

One-another ministry is done through informal relationships. The reason the helpee pursues the helper has more to do with trust, respect, and availability than education, experience, or expertise. The hub of this type of care is usually small groups, ministry teams, or shared life activities. It is natural, appropriate, and beneficial for the helper and helpee (roles that are not well defined at this level) to exchange phone numbers, mingle with each other's families, and have other casual social interactions.

Level of Training

The preaching and discipleship ministries of a church provide the training for one-another ministry. Whether effective or ineffective, this is where the content, tone, and culture for each church's one-another ministry is established.

There is no formal training for one-another care. No one gets a doctorate degree in friendship, a master's degree in accountability, or becomes licensed in encouragement. The qualifications for one-another care are simply being liked and trusted enough for someone to share their hardship with you.

If you want to enrich the one-another culture of your church in a way that is compatible with this book, consider having your small groups study another book in this Church-Based Counseling series: *Transformative Friendships: 7 Simple Questions to Deepen Any Relationship.*[2]

Level of Experience

The experience level of one-another care varies widely, based upon the helper's age, personal history, number of years as a Christian, type of education, vocational background, etc. The most valuable qualities for one-another ministry are longevity of relationship and accessibility. If the individual seeking help has needs that require expertise instead of longevity of friendship, then one-another ministry should not be the exclusive form of care they receive.

Advantages and Opportunities

One-another ministry is highly replicable and readily available, and it occurs within a context of lasting relationship between the people involved. One-another ministry happens naturally without artificial pairing. For this reason, a church may enhance its one-another ministry, but it doesn't launch a friendship ministry.

One-another ministry is informal (i.e., meeting in a coffee shop or living room, without case notes, and with limited role definition). The absence of formality allows the stigma often associated with counseling to be avoided. It also alleviates liability concerns that emerge for a church when counseling becomes more formal.

---

2. Brad Hambrick, *Transformative Friendships: 7 Simple Questions to Deepen Any Relationship* (Greensboro, NC: New Growth Press, 2024).

Limitations and Weaknesses

It is often hard for those who do not have preexisting relationships within a church to find one-another care during a time of crisis or emotional distress. Either the individual in need of care waits for friendship to develop naturally before sharing their struggle (resulting in a long delay in receiving care), or their struggle becomes the basis of a young relationship (resulting in one-way relationships that are less sustainable for the helper).

In one-another care, the helper's personal experience and favorite Bible passages or Christian books can overly influence the advice given. Anecdotal examples of "what worked for me" or "what comes to my mind" can result in a higher rate of well-intended but ineffective advice than more experienced helpers would give.

Also, those providing one-another care vary in their comfort level when talking about emotional or relational struggles. In one-another ministry, the helpers didn't know they were agreeing to be helpers when the relationship began, so they may feel like difficult conversations are more than they signed up for. If the helper is uncomfortable, it can be hurtful to the person seeking help.

While one-another care has many advantages, we need to be mindful of these limitations and look for ways to provide supplemental care when needed. These kinds of limitations motivate churches to desire a counseling ministry; hence, you picked up this book.

IMPORTANT TRANSITION BETWEEN LEVEL ONE AND LEVEL TWO

A major transition occurs as we move from one-another care to more formal levels of counseling. When a church's care moves beyond one-another ministry, artificial pairing necessarily occurs. **Artificial pairing** occurs when

- a *request* for counseling is made by the helpee;
- the *church recommends* a helper or ministry that is not a natural part of the helpee's life; and
- the helpee comes to the helper with the *expectation* that counsel provided will be from someone who is more than just a friend.

When a church facilitates an artificial pairing, the church has a responsibility to both the helper and the helpee. **For the helper**, the church should ensure that

- there is a reasonable opportunity for success on the part of the helper, and
- the helpee comes with an accurate understanding of type of counsel being provided.

A church should know the scope of care of its counseling ministry and only recommend individuals to that ministry who are a good fit for what it provides.

To the helpee, the church should provide clear information about

- the type of care a given ministry provides,
- the level of training a counselor or ministry leader has,
- the type of curriculum or activity that will be involved in the counseling process, and
- an estimate of the duration of the helping relationship.

This requires clear information on a church's website, a well-informed staff member who responds to counseling inquiries, and quality intake forms for level-three counseling and higher.

LEVEL TWO: G4, GCM, AND COMPARABLE MINISTRIES

Level-two counseling ministries are what you might call "lay counseling light." The relationships established are more than friendships. The helper and helpee are artificially paired, and they follow a course of care provided by a curriculum. However, the counseling process doesn't yet take on elements of formality such as meeting by appointment, using intake forms, or taking case notes.

Scope of Ministry

G4 allows the group facilitator to care for up to twelve participants at the same time. GCM allows the mentors to care for one or more couples at a time and still be meaningfully involved in other ministries of the church. As we saw in chapter 8, these features are important for the long-term sustainability of a church-based counseling ministry.

Level of Training

For training in leading counseling groups, G4 facilitators have worked through *Facilitating*, and they have gained familiarity with the subject-specific curriculum of their group. *Facilitating* also contains guidance on how to use curriculums written by other authors within a G4 ministry.

GCM mentors have been through the mentor training at brad-hambrick.com/gcm and work through the relevant portions of the *Creating a Gospel-Centered Marriage* materials as they meet with their engaged couples.

Level of Experience

G4 and GCM leaders rely heavily upon their personal experience for credibility (see chapter 14). However, their curriculum and training help them differentiate lessons that are anecdotal and personal ("I found this helpful") from overarching principles and key aspects of assessment that are vital to helping their group members or mentees succeed in overcoming whatever struggles they are facing.

The quality of level two or level-three counseling ministries is enhanced when the director of these ministries has the opportunity to consult with a level-four counselor as difficult situations arise. Chapters 16 and 17 discuss how to identify a consultant like this in your community and provide guidance for a good working relationship with this counseling consultant.

Advantages and Opportunities

First, level-two ministries are excellent expressions of 2 Corinthians 1:3–5 as believers share the comfort and wisdom they have received from God with others. Second, these ministries can serve the church and community free of charge. The only costs associated with these ministries are usually the curriculum guides.

In addition, these ministries can be effective forms of outreach, especially in communities that are under-resourced. Because G4 and

GCM are built on biblical principles and contain a clear process for assimilation of participants into the life of the church, these ministries can be simultaneously effective at caring for people with acute needs (short-term) and helping people see the benefits of church life as God's long-term design for growth and support.

Limitations and Weaknesses

Each church will be dependent upon the experience of its members to determine what topics it can address. If the lay leaders for these ministries are not also gifted in leadership or administration, the ability of these ministries to expand beyond a single group or set of mentors can be limited.

A risk of a recovery group ministry is that as it grows, it can sometimes turn into a church within a church. If the level of transparency within the counseling ministry is greater than the level of transparency within the general church culture, those in the counseling ministry can begin to feel like they are the ones really doing church. For this reason, when a church launches a counseling ministry, its discipleship ministry needs to take simultaneous steps to increase the authenticity within the congregation generally. (*Transformative Friendships*, recommended earlier, can help with this.)

Furthermore, when a church begins a formal counseling ministry at level two or higher, it needs to consult with its insurance provider. Areas of consultation could include the need for increased liability insurance, coverage for volunteers, and any best practices guidelines to reduce liability. Questions and guidance for this conversation are included in chapter 19.

Note: From this point forward, we will define types of counseling ministries that lie outside the scope of this book, so we will cover them more briefly. However, this discussion of more formal models of counseling will provide categories that enable you to articulate the difference between what G4 and GCM offer and what potential participants or church leaders might mistakenly assume is offered.

LEVEL THREE: EDUCATED COUNSELOR

A lay counselor in a level-three ministry is meeting with individuals, couples, or families by appointment. The counseling ministry looks like a miniature counseling center within a local church. The counselee completes intake forms with an extensive personal history and receives an explanation of policies. The counselor takes notes during sessions, creates counseling objectives, and develops some type of treatment plan with each counselee.

Scope of Ministry

In a level-three ministry, a counselor is expected to be able to address a greater variety and complexity of life struggles than a layperson in a level-two ministry. By contrast, in G4 and GCM, the name of the group or ministry specifies the struggles or life transitions that participants are seeking help with.

Level three is the muddy middle that church leaders often think of when they envision launching a counseling ministry. The level of formality is high, but the counselor's level of experience in a formal setting is low. And few lay counseling training programs provide instruction on the responsibilities that come with receiving privileged information. The result of this lack of experience and training is that this is the level at which a church is most likely to make mistakes that incur liability.

Level of Training

In a church, the training for level-three counselors is usually a certification program. There are many parachurch organizations and theological seminaries that provide certifications for lay counseling. The hours of instruction, quantity of reading, and amount of experience required for most of these certification programs is the equivalent of one or two graduate-level seminary classes. Students in such programs receive a first-aid level of counseling instruction for a wide variety of life struggles. No one subject is delved into at great length because of the time limitations.

However, the credential the lay counselor holds—certification—is not always well understood by the counselee. It is easy for counselees to mistake a lay certification as being commensurate with the licensure of a professional counselor. For this reason, churches need to be clear in their informed consent process about the differences between types of counselors.

Level of Experience

In the secular equivalents for this level of counseling, a counselor is not allowed to counsel without supervision until they reach 1,500 to 3,000 hours of experience (the number varies based upon the type of license and the state in which a counselor practices). In contrast, certification programs, at the time of this publication, require only 50 supervised hours. This difference in supervised client contact hours is why level-four counselors are given the title "experienced" to differentiate them from level-three counselors.

Advantages and Opportunities

Having this type of counseling in a local church increases the amount of individualized care that is available for its members and community. Offering these types of ministries within a church can counter the stigma that comes with the frequently held assumption that "If I were a good Christian, then I wouldn't have emotional or relational struggles." Eliminating this stigma benefits the entire discipleship culture of a church.

Limitations and Weaknesses

This level of counseling does not have the benefit of easy accessibility that level-one and level-two ministries have. This is due to both the time restrictions of formal counseling and the limited caseload a lay counselor can handle. Furthermore, for a level-three lay counseling ministry, it is highly recommended that a church have an experienced counselor (level four) on staff. Otherwise, the liability from lack of quality supervision can outweigh the benefits.

LEVEL FOUR: EXPERIENCED COUNSELOR

An experienced counselor, who could also be called a general practitioner, is someone with both the education and extensive experience to serve people with a wide variety of counseling concerns.

Scope of Ministry

A level-four counselor is not necessarily competent to address any life struggle; rather, good general practitioners readily acknowledge their limitations. They will refer a counselee to another counselor when their training, experience, or setting does not serve that counselee well.

Level of Training

Level-four counselors have completed at least a master's degree in counseling and have between 3,000 and 10,000 hours of counseling experience. General practitioners are continuing their education through reading, conferences, and counselor consultations to increase their skill and areas of competence.

Level of Experience

Between level three and four is a shift in how experience is measured. In level three, counselors track their total number of counseling hours. As a counselor reaches level four, they begin to track how many cases or hours they have worked at addressing specific life struggles (depression with suicidal ideations, anxiety involving panic attacks, eating disorders, etc.). At level four, a counselor grows in comfort with both the counseling process (interviewing, assessment, gauging counselee commitment, recognizing ethical dilemmas, determining the pace of counseling, etc.) and competence with specific life struggles.

Advantages and Opportunities

An experienced counselor should be able to assess and triage the importance of a counselee's primary struggle(s), determine which approaches are likely to be most effective for each struggle, and explain recommendations clearly in light of possible alternatives. This experience level increases the trust of a counselee and thereby improves counseling effectiveness.

Limitations and Weaknesses

For many churches or individuals, the costs that emerge at level four prevent access to counseling. Some churches might envision a level-four helper as a pastor of counseling who serves as a counselor for a retainer fee. However, that model presents significant sustainability challenges. A good counselor providing free services will generate a long waiting list and, thereby, disgruntlement among church members who are unable to get an appointment in a timely manner.

LEVEL FIVE: COUNSELING SPECIALIST

A counseling specialist is competent to counsel severe cases of a particular struggle or is making a unique contribution to the development of counseling.

Scope of Ministry

As a supervisor, teacher, or author, a counseling specialist is working to advance the ability of the church to minister effectively in their area of expertise.

Level of Training

A specialist is advancing the field in their area of expertise. Their study and observations are becoming the curriculum for level three and four counselors. Critical feedback on their work from peers and those utilizing their materials serves as a refining mechanism for their work.

Level of Experience

There is no standard number of hours a counselor must log to be considered a specialist; it is impossible to quantify the number of hours required to gain mastery in a subject area or skill. However, 10,000 hours of experience is often cited as the minimum number required to achieve true expertise, as neurologist Daniel Levitin states:

The emerging picture from such studies is that ten thousand hours of practice is required to achieve the level of mastery associated with being a world-class expert—in anything. In study after study, of composers, basketball players, fiction writers, ice skaters, concert pianists, chess players, master criminals, and what have you, this number comes up again and again. . . . No one has yet found a case in which true world-class expertise was accomplished in less time.[3]

Advantages and Opportunities

Two major advantages and opportunities emerge with this level of competence. First, a specialist provides an excellent quality of care for those who need more than general counseling. Second, through writing and teaching, specialists advance the ability of the church to minister well in their area of expertise.

Limitations and Weaknesses

Availability is the predominant weakness of the specialist model. This problem arises both because of the limited number of hours any individual can counsel per week and because of geographic limitations. There will not be a specialist for every issue in every city.

CONCLUSION

We've just covered a lot of ground. I don't want you to feel overwhelmed by all this information, so I'd like to offer two words of encouragement as you leave this chapter and carry on with our journey.

First, if you can more clearly articulate how a level-two counseling ministry (in our case, G4 and GCM) differs from both level one (friendship) and level three (miniature counseling centers), you have gotten everything you need from this chapter. Don't let the other information distract you.

Second, *be excellent where you are.* The danger in talking about levels of competence is the assumption that "higher is better." That

---

3. Daniel Levitin, *This Is Your Brain on Music* (New York: Penguin, 2007), 193. See also Malcolm Gladwell, *Outliers* (New York: Little, Brown and Company, 2008).

is the kind of misconception that could lead us to think paid clergy are better Christians than laypeople. Knowing both the advantages and the limitations of your level of care allows you to hold the proper balance between humility (i.e., we won't and can't do everything) and confidence (i.e., we can do some really important and impactful things).

If your church currently offers only level-one care, be excited about that and excellent at it. Enrich it. As you consider creating level-two ministries like G4 and GCM, understand what is entailed in launching those well. There is also a great deal of good that can be done through these ministries.

As you help lead your church to do what it can do with excellence, many people will see their lives changed in profound ways while many members get to use their life experiences to bless others. Many family trees will be radically reshaped for the better because of your faithfulness to do what you can with excellence.

Chapter 10

WHERE IS THE PASTOR IN THIS MODEL?

If one of the core values for a level-two counseling ministry is being *church compatible*, we must ask, "Where is the pastor?" So far, we haven't talked much about the pastor. This is awkward because it's likely that up to this point in your church's life, most of the counseling at your church has been done by your pastor—at least in any formal sense of the word.

When we ask, "Where is the pastor in a G4 or GCM model?," it can refer to physical presence, level of engagement with the ministry, or access to information. We will look at all three topics because each provides a helpful perspective on what the role of a pastor could be—and shouldn't be—in the lay counseling ministry you are preparing to launch. Consider the following summary questions:

1. How and where does counseling done by a pastor fit in this model?
2. What role should a pastor play in this kind of lay counseling ministry?
3. What access should a pastor have to information disclosed in this type of counseling?

In this chapter, I will use the word *pastor* in the singular to refer not just to a senior pastor but to anyone on the pastoral staff. And the information given here about pastors will in many churches also apply to elders or other leaders that a church formally recognizes as having shepherding responsibilities over the congregation.

COUNSELING BY THE PASTOR

How does pastoral counseling fit into these models? Does having a counseling ministry serve the Acts 6 function of removing counseling from a pastor's plate? We will answer both yes and no.

If you are familiar with Acts 6:1–6, you know that it explains how the role of deacon was established in the early church. The apostles were administratively overwhelmed by benevolence needs—the care of widows—to the point that they could not give adequate attention to their prayer and teaching responsibilities.

Ask yourself, "In Acts 6, after deacons were created, did that mean the apostles (an by extension pastors) no longer cared for widows?" The obvious answer is no. It meant that other leaders in the church—the deacons—bore the responsibility to ensure there was an overarching care plan. Each deacon would have had a list of the church's widows and their needs to coordinate care.

But the pastors still pastored widows; that is, they prayed with them, taught them, shared meals with them, etc. The pastors pastored the widows in the same manner and in the same rhythms as they pastored the other church members. The emergence of this new role simply meant that the acute care was managed by the deacons.

Similarly, having G4 and GCM at your church means that there will be a growing number of members providing intensive care for brothers and sisters who need it. But those ministries do not replace your pastors. Pastors still shepherd those who are participating in the counseling ministry, but they relate to them in pastoral ways rather than providing acute care.

Now we are left asking, "How does the care provided through private conversations with a pastor differ from the care provided through G4 and GCM?" To answer this question, we must clarify the categories we use for the types of shepherding work a pastor does.[1] In making this clarification, we need to bear two things in mind. First, as we have seen, counseling is a broad term, so we'll need to be clear about what we mean when we speak of "pastoral counseling." Second, when we clarify types of care (as we did in chapter 9), we are not ranking them; we are merely removing as much confusion as possible.

David Benner provides a three-fold distinction between pastoral ministry, pastoral care, and pastoral counseling that can help us find the clarity we are seeking.[2] Think of these as nested laundry baskets into which we are sorting various pastoral responsibilities.

This diagram captures how broad pastoral ministry to the congregation results in the opportunity to provide more narrow care for individuals or families. As pastors do broad work well, they become aware of more individual needs, for which the pastors do not have

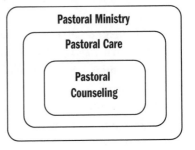

the capacity—either time or expertise—to provide all the subsequent care needed. In a broken world, there is always more need than hours in a pastor's week.

Here are descriptions of the three categories of pastoral work shown in the diagram, moving from broad to specific:

- **Pastoral ministry** is what pastors do for *the congregation as a whole or for subgroups of the congregation*: preaching (including sermon prep), teaching, leading worship, leading committees or work groups, leading ministry teams, advising small-group leaders, etc.

---

1. The section below is a modified excerpt from lesson two of my free, eight-part, online resource *The Pastor as Counselor*, which can be found at bradhambrick.com/pastorascounselor.
2. Modified and adapted from David Benner, *Strategic Pastoral Counseling* (Grand Rapids: Baker, 1998), 14–15.

- **Pastoral care** is *ministry at the pastor's initiative with individuals or families*: visiting the sick and homebound, reaching out to families during seasons of grief or tragedy, praying for church members, encouraging volunteer leaders, enacting church discipline, etc.
- **Pastoral counseling** is ministry done *in response to a member's request that is focused on giving guidance to someone facing a particular life struggle*. This is the part of a pastor's work that most overlaps with the ministries you are preparing to launch.

One goal for starting a counseling ministry is to allow pastors to devote more time to pastoral ministry and pastoral care by taking on many (though not all) of the church's counseling needs. Pastors are finite human beings who live within the confines of a 168-hour week. Acts 6-like ministries are essential for pastors to thrive and churches to function well.

Good pastoral ministry and pastoral care are going to result in people bringing their emotional and relational struggles to their pastors. This is good. Even with a thriving and robust counseling ministry, you want this to continue.

The pastor may choose to counsel some of these individuals personally, but the pastor will not have the capacity to care for everyone individually for as long as they need. Pastors need to be able to point people to other care options either inside or outside the church.[3] The ministry you are creating is a way to increase the options available within your church.

So, now we narrow this first question one more time and ask, "What unique role do pastors play that helps us determine when it is best for them to take on the role of pastoral counseling for a particular individual?" If pastors don't have the capacity to provide all the care asked of them, there should be some criteria to help them make this decision in a way that is principled, rather than arbitrary.

---

3. Chapter 17 provides instructions on how to create a referral list, guidance on when it is wise to make a referral, and recommendations for building a two-way relationship with these referral resources (i.e., you utilize their services to benefit participants in your ministries, and they recommend your G4 and GCM ministries to clients).

Let's engage this question by looking at what ministries like G4 and GCM do and don't provide. G4 and GCM do provide a place to process a particular hardship or major life transition. These ministries do not serve a pastoral function; in other words, no one in these ministries takes on the leadership role or doctrinal responsibilities of a pastor. Let me illustrate these principles using a chart with examples.

G4 and GCM do... (Counseling Functions)	G4 and GCM do not... (Pastoral Functions)
Help someone process a divorce	Determine the church's position on remarriage
Help someone respond in God-honoring ways when they are angry	Decide whether someone with a history of anger should be leading a small group
Help someone pursue sexual purity	Decide if church discipline is needed or when the restoration process is complete
Provide premarital preparation and mentoring	Decide whether the pastor should officiate a wedding for a couple with red flags in their relationship

The second column gives examples of pastoral counseling that a lay counseling ministry cannot replace. The first column illustrates ways that a lay counseling ministry effectively provides an Acts 6-like relief valve for the time-consuming care needed within the church.

THE ROLE OF THE PASTOR IN A COUNSELING MINISTRY

Let's continue our reflection on the finitude of pastors. Much of what leads to pastoral burnout (and the subsequent crises in churches) is a result of pastors doing more than God called them to do. By removing from a pastor's workload things that lay leaders can do equally well, a lay counseling ministry facilitates pastoral health and longevity.

And what constitutes the essential work of a pastor? Ephesians 4:11–12 gives us one of the clearest New Testament articulations of what God wants pastors to do:

And he [Jesus] gave the apostles, the prophets, the evange-
lists, the shepherds and teachers, to equip the saints for the
work of ministry, for building up the body of Christ.

We see that God intends church leaders to "equip" church members to do "the work of ministry" so that the people are cared for
and built up. God did not design the church to be a place where
professional Christians were hired to take care of all the members.
God designed the church to be a place of mutual care between members mobilized by pastors. The work of equipping and mobilizing is
the primary, functional role of pastors in the lay counseling model
espoused in this book.

What does it look like for pastors to "equip" a counseling ministry? Pastoral equipping means providing the kind of support necessary for ministries like G4 and GCM to thrive. This includes:

- Knowing the church membership well enough to identify
  potential leaders.
- Being aware of the needs in the church well enough to recommend potential participants.
- Praying for and encouraging the leaders of this ministry as
  they care for others.
- Creating awareness of the ministry within the congregation.
- Engaging the exclusively pastoral needs that emerge from G4
  and GCM (like those in column two of the chart above) so volunteers do not feel like their efforts are incomplete.

These are the sustainable expectations for a pastor in a church
with a lay counseling ministry. If a church has multiple pastors, it
should be clear which pastor is primarily responsible for oversight
and encouragement of G4 and GCM. Otherwise, when a responsibility belongs to everyone, it actually belongs to no one.

PASTORAL ACCESS TO COUNSELING INFORMATION

This kind of involvement from a pastor—directly encouraging leaders—pushes us to ask one of the stickiest questions for a lay counseling

ministry: how much access should the pastor have to the information shared *in* the counseling ministry? If we don't communicate clearly and act consistently at this point, a counseling ministry becomes a hornet's nest of hurt feelings and liability.

As a helpful parallel, consider the information people share in a church's counseling ministry like the money people give in a church's offering. Churches recognize that different monetary gifts may need to be treated differently. A designated gift to the building fund has certain legal restrictions (i.e., it can only be used for the building). General tithes aren't similarly restricted. Both designated gifts and general tithes should be documented for tax deduction purposes. But buying a plate of barbecue dinner to support the youth going to camp doesn't provide the same tax deduction because something of value was received in return for the money.

In the paragraph above, you'll notice that the *same commodity* (i.e., money) given by the *same person* may be treated differently by the *same church* based on how, when, by whom, and why it was received. The same is true for people's personal information. Context matters. Not every tearful conversation is counseling. Talking to a friend after small group about a marital conflict is different from sharing the same story in an anger group. The context in which something is shared determines the restrictions on sharing that information. Understanding these distinctions becomes increasingly important as a church develops a more formal counseling ministry. Section two will walk you through these kinds of distinctions in greater detail. For now, it's enough that you understand the importance of recognizing the difference in information shared inside or outside your counseling ministry.

If you have a clear grasp of the limits of both pastors and counseling ministries, and if you're able to see how pastors and counseling ministries can serve and encourage one another, you have the foundation for a fruitful partnership that will result in the building up of the church.

Chapter 11

TEN CHALLENGES: WHY WOULDN'T WE WANT A COUNSELING MINISTRY?

f I summarized this chapter in three words, they would be "eyes wide open."

Every ministry that a church offers adds some burdens. There is no such thing as a ministry that is all perks and no challenges. A counseling ministry, even with the advantages we're striving to create with the design of G4 and GCM, is no different. And because it is less common than, say, a youth ministry, the challenges can be more difficult to identify. We are called to be sober minded in our individual lives as Christians (Romans 12:3), and the same principle is relevant for the ministries we launch as a church.

The goal for this chapter is to put some of the commonly unforeseen challenges into words. At times in this chapter you may feel like I am trying to talk you out of starting a counseling ministry. I am not, but I am trying to ensure that you have thought through the probable challenges ahead. Why? Because we are most prone to make mistakes that hurt people and result in liability when we are reacting to things we didn't anticipate.

Unfortunately, understanding these challenges does not eliminate them. While you can mitigate their prevalence, these ten challenges are realities that will exist if you have a counseling ministry. When you start formalizing counseling at your church, you need to decide whether the benefits are worth the hardships. That is the reason I will also discuss the advantages that emerge when we face each challenge well.

1. A COUNSELING MINISTRY WILL NOT DO EVERYTHING, SO YOU WILL STILL MAKE REFERRALS.

Your church's counseling ministry will not have a specific group or mentoring relationship for every life struggle. In addition, some struggles will be more severe than can be handled effectively via G4 or GCM. A key premise of leading a counseling ministry that is liability wise is *do what you can do well, know your limits, and grow as you are able to do so wisely.*

The pastoral leadership at your church needs to understand that you will not be able to serve every person who requests counseling. They cannot send just anyone to the new counseling ministry to take care of it.

When the counseling ministry says, "We are not equipped to meet the need for which you are seeking help," it is not saying, "This church won't care for you." It is saying that the church is equipped to offer level-one friendship care, but not level-two counseling. The church can always provide one-another care and pastoral care, but a lay counseling ministry must know its limits and stay within them.

Advantage: If managed and networked well, a counseling ministry can serve as a connection point to both community resources that provide need-specific counseling and discipleship ministries of the church for one-another care. A caring response to someone reaching out for a trauma group at a church that doesn't have a trauma group might sound like this:

> We greatly appreciate you trusting us enough to reach out for help. Currently, we do not have a G4 group for trauma. We do know several counselors in our area who are experienced at counseling trauma that we can recommend to you. As a church, we still want to come alongside you. We can connect you with one of our pastors who can provide pastoral support and help you find a small group that meets for

general discipleship and encouragement. As a church, even when we can't provide counseling, we still want to provide friendship and support.

You will notice in this vignette that the counseling ministry did not directly connect this person to a small group. If a leader of the counseling ministry connected this person with a small group leader, this would over-disclose that this person requested counseling. That's why, in this vignette, the counseling ministry offered to connect them to a pastor (honoring whether this is a step the individual wanted to take) for a more natural connection with a small group. This is an example of the right way to handle the vulnerable information that is frequently disclosed to a counseling ministry.

2. A COUNSELING MINISTRY BECOMES A LIGHTNING ROD FOR HARD CASES AND INTERPERSONAL CONFLICTS.

Things that are unresolved find their way to counseling. If you have groups for addiction, betrayal, or processing the experience of abuse (just to pick three), individuals experiencing these types of crises will often reach out to your church for help. Both during and after their crises, these individuals will come to expect that the church can help them with the interpersonal fallout.

For example, if the wife of a husband caught in sexual addiction finds help through the *True Betrayal* G4 group, she will no longer be hurting in silence. This is good. But she will begin to ask, "Why is my husband still a member in good standing?" or "Will the church support me if I pursue divorce because of his repeated infidelities?" These questions move the matter from the counseling ministry (processing personal experience) to the pastors and elders of the church. The more effective the church's counseling ministry, the more these types of situations will emerge.

Advantage: These situations already exist. Having a counseling ministry does not create them. But an effective counseling ministry provides the advantage of allowing these situations to be handled in stages (i.e., processing the personal experience first, and then navigating the interpersonal challenges). When someone is in the early stages of processing their pain, it is often hard for them to also have the emotional bandwidth to address the interpersonal fallout. If situations like the one above are only handled via pastoral counseling, where the pastor has responsibilities for both husband and wife, he attempts to help resolve both the personal pain and interpersonal fallout at the same time. Even if the early stages are handled well via pastoral counseling, few pastors can invest the time necessary to be the primary caregiver in the middle and later stages of care.

3. A COUNSELING MINISTRY WILL BE MISREPRESENTED AND CARICATURED BY THOSE WHO DISLIKE THE COUNSEL THEY RECEIVE.

Not everyone who participates in counseling will find their experience helpful. This is true for both professional and lay counseling, Christian and secular. Those who do not find their experience helpful are prone to blame the counselor, sometimes rightly, but other times by misrepresenting the counsel they received.

Due to the constraints of confidentiality, the counselor and church are limited in their ability to defend themselves against these critical remarks. The same parameters that make counseling a safe place for heightened honesty and vulnerability also make it more difficult to protect the ministry from disparagement.

Advantage: The fact that both G4 and GCM are based on curriculum allows your church to be transparent about the content of what is counseled without disclosing specifics of an individual's story. This is an advantage that does not exist when lay counselors are operating as general practitioners and developing a care plan (i.e., developing their own content) for each counseling relationship.

4. A COUNSELING MINISTRY WILL ATTRACT SITUATIONS IN WHICH SAFETY CONCERNS AND LEGAL REQUIREMENTS ARE AT THE FOREFRONT OF DECISION-MAKING.

With a counseling ministry, a church is asking to be involved in more situations involving abuse, suicidal ideations, and other problems in which the immediate well-being of the counselee is the forefront concern. In these situations, the threat to the individual's body (i.e., life and safety) makes the care of their soul (i.e., character, beliefs, and values) secondary. Church members are often uncomfortable when the needs of an individual flip our default, soul-first mentality.

Regardless of whether a church has a counseling ministry or not, their staff and key leaders should have completed an educational track like *Becoming a Church that Cares Well for the Abused*[1] to learn how to respond to reports of abuse. It is vital for all churches to know when abuse reporting is mandated, to whom the report should be made, what happens after a report is made, and how to care well even when reporting is not mandated. The need for such knowledge will become more frequent when your church has a counseling ministry.

Advantage: Having a counseling ministry forces a church to think through issues like mandated reporting or suicide response *prior to* a crisis event. The time to get educated on these matters is not in the middle of a crisis. If creating a counseling ministry prompts a church leadership team to think through these issues more thoroughly, the counseling ministry will have served the church well before it meets with its first counselee.

5. A COUNSELING MINISTRY WILL ATTRACT SITUATIONS IN WHICH YOUR PASTORS ARE NOT EXPERTS.

If you have a support group for depression, choices regarding psychotropic medications will be discussed. If you have a support group for destructive relationships, questions about gauging change and safety after domestic violence will emerge. If you have a support group for addiction, then questions will arise about whether residential care is needed. These are just a few examples of situations that regularly come up in counseling and about which Christians often have strong opinions, but which are not areas in which most pastors have expertise.

In difficult situations like these, a good counseling ministry doesn't tell people what to do. It advises them to consult with the relevant professionals (psychiatrists, social workers, addiction specialists, attorneys, etc.) and provides a safe place for them to process the advice of these professionals in light of their Christian values.

---

1. This book and teaching videos from the authors can be found at churchcares.com.

Advantage: These situations require pastors and other church leaders to express healthy humility and learn from experts in other disciplines. They also provide an opportunity for pastors to shepherd the congregation in how to honor the personal autonomy of others, even when they disagree with a wisdom decision they are making (and this means recognizing that not every choice is a moral issue). Learning from experts in other fields is an excellent way to bring nuance and a tender, humble tone to the way difficult subjects like mental health, addiction, and abuse are addressed in a church's preaching and teaching ministries.

6. A COUNSELING MINISTRY DEALS WITH CHALLENGES ON WHICH YOUR CHURCH DOES NOT HAVE AN OFFICIAL STANCE.

Is there a biblical statute of limitations on when a spouse can opt for divorce after infidelity? Can a church require someone to pursue counseling if it's needed but not wanted? Are the outbursts related to a trigger response from trauma the same as those from selfish anger? How responsible is someone for the grandiose and immoral actions they commit during a manic episode? As a church engages with people asking these kinds of questions via the counseling ministry, these topics will come up more frequently in pastoral care.

The instinct of many pastors and elders is to lead from the church's official positions. But this practice becomes more difficult to maintain as the church delves deeper into the brokenness of human experience. A church won't have an official position on all these questions and the myriad of other questions that will emerge. Pastors will be required to develop a more robust skill set of walking alongside people making wisdom decisions, rather than evaluating choices exclusively in moral categories.

Advantage: These new skills of care are vital for holistic pastoral care. Too often, hard decisions are oversimplified with the belief that the experts *out there* don't agree with our theology. Sometimes external experts do have views that conflict with fundamental beliefs of the church. But often they are just approaching the same subject with different questions. Having a ministry that grapples with these things in theologically responsible ways helps prevent a church from artificially simplifying multidimensional questions. As pastors become humble learners alongside church members, rather than just teachers, they become better shepherds.

7. PROMOTING A COUNSELING MINISTRY CAN BE A CHALLENGE BECAUSE COUNSELING DOES NOT HAVE A SPECIFIC DEMOGRAPHIC LIKE OTHER MINISTRY AREAS.

Most ministries serve a distinct population—children, youth, young professionals, seniors, etc. People know whether they belong to the group based upon demographic factors, and they are not offended when they receive an invitation to participate in that ministry. For example, it's not problematic for a parent to receive an email that says, "We know you have a middle school student, so you will want to know..." The church can be sure that only parents with middle school students get this communication.

Churches try to limit their congregation-wide communications so that they don't overwhelm their people and inadvertently teach them to ignore promotions sent from the church. If you have ever been in church leadership, you know the intense negotiations for what makes it into the Sunday morning announcements. So, in order to generate and maintain awareness, ministries must use other communication channels. But this doesn't work well for a counseling ministry. Trying to narrow communication for the counseling ministry to only those who need it is offensive. The response might be, "Why are you sending *me* an invitation to join the church's new group for addicts?"

Further, no one feels awkward if you publicly promote youth camp, worship team auditions, or the next mission trip, but people can get uncomfortable if you mention sexual addiction or a group for those in destructive relationships. They may ask, "Why are we starting these groups? How are we defining those terms?" So, it is both more necessary (for awareness) and more difficult (for clarity) to communicate about the church's counseling ministry.

Advantage: Your church will be challenged to think creatively about communication. Keeping the counseling page on your church website updated and clear will be important. The church's social media platforms provide a good means of communication because people usually access these via the privacy of their phones. This allows you to include links to more information, which would be cumbersome in a verbal announcement.

8. HAVING A COUNSELING MINISTRY WILL ATTRACT IDEAS FOR NEW MINISTRIES YOU MAY NOT WANT.

When you create the infrastructure for a new type of ministry, people are going to bring you their ideas. Creating a structure like G4 is no different. People get excited about whatever they have found helpful. This means that when they bring ideas for a group curriculum the G4 ministry could use, they are going to be very passionate about it. After all, it changed their life.

You may get requests to lead a prayer group for deliverance from addiction, a group for individuals experiencing same-sex attraction that claims to make participants heterosexual, or an educational group that claims that mental illness is a harmful myth. Your church will have to decide which groups and which curriculum can be a part of your counseling ministry.

Advantage: You may become aware of a good curriculum you did not know existed. You will become aware of needs that your members feel are underserved in the church. You will also learn more about where your people are already turning for help. Resolving questions about which curriculum to utilize in your counseling ministry will take time, but it is well-spent time and provides an opportunity to disciple those who are making the request.

9. A COUNSELING MINISTRY WILL CREATE CONFUSION ABOUT WHAT YOUR PASTORS, SMALL GROUP LEADERS, AND LAY COUNSELORS DO.

We began addressing the issue of roles in chapters 9 and 10. But this issue is one that you will be perpetually clarifying with your members and church staff. This is because *counseling* is such a broad term. We can't change the breadth of ways our members use the word *counseling*, but we can be intentional about clarifying how we use the term *counseling* to describe our ministry.

Once you start a counseling ministry, you want to continually be doing three things: (1) increasing the quality of one-another care in your general discipleship ministries, (2) providing your congregation with as much pastoral care as possible by your staff and elders, and (3) launching new G4 groups to allow your church to care with greater excellence for people with specific needs. As you expand the number of options in this third category, it will inevitably create confusion about the first two.

Advantage: This can force a church, both leaders and congregants, to get better at articulating "this is what a [ministry / role] can do well." There is only so much a small group leader can do well. There is only so much a pastor can do well. Creating a counseling ministry is a way to acknowledge that there are limits to these two forms of ministry. A church culture that can acknowledge the limits of what it does well is a healthier church culture.

10. A COUNSELING MINISTRY IN A SMALL TO MID-SIZED CHURCH CAN CHANGE THE PERSONALITY OF THAT CHURCH.

This point is not meant to imply that larger churches are better. It merely acknowledges that thirty people are 30 percent of a one-hundred-member church, and 3 percent of a one-thousand-member church. The same thirty people are going to have a different degree of impact on the culture of either of these two churches. This influence, however, won't come about because this group of thirty people set out to change the church culture. Rather, this influence will occur naturally as a result of their mere presence and of what they find most impactful about their experience of church.

A counseling ministry focused on groups and mentoring will necessarily be niche-oriented. Thus, it will attract people with a shared life struggle (addiction, divorce, depression, etc.) or life transition (becoming engaged, experiencing grief, starting a blended family). As a result, the new people that a counseling ministry attracts are focused more specifically on overcoming a particular struggle, rather than more broadly growing as a disciple. This will impact the culture of the church.

Further, participants in a counseling ministry must grow in their level of authenticity and transparency in order to benefit from that ministry. Counseling doesn't work when people aren't honest. If they don't find a comparable level of authenticity and transparency in the general discipleship ministries of the church, they can begin to view the church as superficial.

Advantage: Authenticity should be a part of body life in a church. To the degree that a counseling ministry challenges a church to grow in this area, it serves the discipleship process well. As long as niche ministries do not hamper a sense that the church exists to reach the entire community, the destigmatizing message they bring—that the gospel is for everyone and God wants to begin a relationship with you where you are—is immensely beneficial.

CONCLUSION

Will all ten of these challenges present themselves at your church? Probably not. You know your church, its members, and your community. You probably already have a sense for which of these challenges are most likely to emerge.

But knowing about these potential challenges means that you can be prepared. It allows you to begin important conversations with key leaders or members who would most likely be upset by one or more of these challenges. Having the awareness to raise important conversations in advance is an essential part of garnering the confidence from your congregation and pastoral leadership to make a ministry like G4 or GCM viable for your church.

Chapter 12

PROBLEMS IN LIVING, MEANING OF LIFE, AND MENTAL HEALTH

In 2014, I had the privilege of serving on the Mental Health Advisory Group (MHAG) for the Southern Baptist Convention. We had more than thirty experts on mental illness: licensed counselors of multiple specialties, psychiatrists, advocates, a neurologist, pastors who specialize in counseling, and social workers. Yet, even with a group like this, we struggled to stay focused on mental illness and not drift into discussing every struggle that comes up in counseling.

Many struggles that find their way to counseling are not mental health concerns: blended families, midlife crises, conflict resolution, life management challenges, pivotal life choices, etc. We realized afresh how many life challenges that are not mental health conditions get discussed in counseling. Each of them is important, but they aren't the reason the MHAG was formed.

Why do I tell you about this? As your church launches a counseling ministry, you are going to face a comparable categorical challenge. What role do your G4 and GCM leaders play in the lives of those they serve? How does this new ministry relate to those professionals who may rightly be involved in the life of someone participating in your counseling ministry?

At this point, you should be able to answer, "We are more than a friend and less than a professional. We provide peer-level care either in the form of a G4 group or GCM mentorship."

But another question can create confusion even when we've been adequately clear about our role. *What kinds of life struggles does this new ministry care for?* In this chapter, we will provide three categories that capture the answer to this question. These three categories aren't as distinct as we might like. For that reason, we will present them using a Venn diagram instead of a columned chart. Life challenges often bridge two, or even all three, categories (hence, the overlapping circles). We shouldn't try to make life simpler than it is just because doing so would make it easier for us to define our new ministry.

Too often, debates about mental health—both inside and outside the church—become heated as someone tries to claim that one of these three circles is the right answer to the question, *What kind of struggle does counseling address?* In other words, their view is that only one of these categories encapsulates everything that gets discussed in counseling. But right versus wrong is a bad framework for this question. It is not a matter of which one captures every experience (i.e., which is right); it is a question of which one(s) best capture the experience of a given individual seeking help (i.e., which fits this person's struggle).

Let's take the example of depression. Which category does it fall into? It could be any of the three or any combination of the three.

Depression is sometimes the result of dysfunction in our brains or glandular systems. That would be *mental illness*. Other times depression results from realizing we've invested our lives in something that just isn't worth it (as happens in a classic midlife crisis). That would be a *meaning of life struggle*. Still other times, depression stems from the hopelessness of a situation, like not knowing how we are going to pay off our mounting debts. That would have a *problems in living* origin.

Here is the primary takeaway for the counseling ministry you are planning to start: *when your church starts a counseling ministry, you are not picking a circle on the Venn diagram.* An aspiration for your ministry is to help members of your church think more clearly about and respond more wisely to the issues that fall within each circle. This is the reason we will explore all three circles.

PROBLEMS IN LIVING

This category is often the most intuitive for those who lead lay counseling ministries. We want to provide practical guidance, rooted in the Bible, for the various challenges people face. Examples of life struggles that fit in this category include time management, self-control, anger management, pornography, debt reduction, stress management, balancing family priorities, conflict resolution, etc.

When we assign a struggle to this category, we are saying that the hardship emerges from our choices, beliefs, or values. What the counselee is doing, believing, or pursuing is causing the life disruption. Counseling in this scenario becomes a highly practical Bible study tailored to the challenges in each counselee's life.

Problems in living is an attractive category for Christians because it aligns with our conception of personal responsibility and doctrine of sin. It is natural for Christians to call each other to own their sin in light of the hope of the gospel. If you took an introduction to psychology course in college, you probably remember a discussion about "personal agency" and the benefits of having an "internal locus of control," more commonly stated, "Change is only possible when we own what we're responsible for." These are three ways of conveying that blame-shifting and excuse-making undermine the change process.

Sin is real. Excuses are bad. When someone's life struggle fits this category, these are wise and important themes to reinforce. We don't need to be ashamed of calling people back to these basic truths. But we also don't need to be a one-tool counseling ministry.

MEANING OF LIFE

This is the category that is most intuitive for theologically and philosophically minded Christians. People whose struggles fall into this category are grappling with the big questions of life and experiencing the disorientation that often hits us when life is hard. Struggles that fit in this category include grief, midlife crises, retirement, intense suffering, and emerging into adulthood as one realizes the weight and responsibility of being a self-sustaining adult.

When we assign a struggle to this category, we are saying that the way a person has made sense of life can no longer account for the challenge they're facing or the demands of the next season of life. There is no way to help people navigate the hardships of life without grappling with the big questions of life, which yields the saying in the biblical counseling world: "Every counselor is a theologian."

The meaning-of-life category is attractive to Christians because it naturally segues into questions of eternal significance. At some level, every life-dominating struggle forces us to ask, "Life can't just be random, so why am I here?" In that same introduction to psychology course, you likely encountered Viktor Frankl, the Auschwitz survivor-turned-therapist who emphasized how important it is to find meaning in life if we are going to survive living in such a broken world. That is what we are doing with the gospel in this category.

We should be excited. This is another meaningful category that is intuitive for Christians to use. But we don't want to stop here. Having two categories is good, and more robust (i.e., theologically accurate) than just one, but the picture is still incomplete.

MENTAL ILLNESS

This category is often less developed than it should be for Christians. We have always believed that the body influences the soul (Matthew 26:41). Good parents know the difference between an upset child who is sleepy or hungry (weak in body) and a child who is being defiant (selfish in will). They know when the child needs a nap, a snack, or correction. That is the distinction we want to make with this third category: when is a problem rooted in our body more than our mind or soul? Remember, we're operating with a Venn diagram; these designations are not all-or-nothing.

When we assign a struggle to the mental illness category, we are saying that the body (often, but not always, the brain) isn't operating as God intended. When this happens, it impacts a person's mood, perception, or response patterns. Examples of life struggles that fit in this category include bipolar disorder, post-traumatic stress, autism spectrum disorder (ASD), obsessive-compulsive disorder (OCD), many experiences of depression or anxiety, and struggles such as schizophrenia that can impact *reality testing* (a technical term for differentiating the objective reality of the external world from one's subjective internal thoughts and emotions).

Mental illness has often been an unappealing category for Christians. We fear it offers an excuse for actions someone should take responsibility for. To date, there are few medical tests to clearly demarcate mental illness. It can seem unclear whether someone is just sad or when they are clinically depressed. A diagnosis of mental illness feels scary, like receiving a diagnosis of Alzheimer's disease. For these and other reasons, Christians have often avoided using this category to classify our life struggles.

This hesitation is understandable. But just because the category is uncomfortable or less clear than we would like doesn't mean it's not valid or useful. When we call something mental illness at the lay level, we're saying two things: (1) The mere passing of time is not going to resolve the struggle and (2) It would be helpful to get assistance from a professional with expertise in this area.

This second point is another source of friction for how people think about a counseling ministry. Is the counseling ministry replacing professional counseling? Are we saying that if you come to this ministry, you don't need to go to a professional? Is the counseling ministry bringing secular teaching into the church? Is the counseling ministry a Trojan horse for psycho heresy to infiltrate the church?

COUNSELING MINISTRY AND PROFESSIONAL COUNSELING

Questions like these are the reason we have devoted an entire chapter to parsing the different types of struggles people bring to counseling. The work we've done in the first twelve chapters should help you answer such questions with more clarity and confidence. It should also position you to be able to consider wisely what kind of help those reaching out to your ministry might need. Understanding how your church's counseling ministry relates to professional counselors in your community is important.

We'll conclude by considering three ways the Venn diagram from this chapter helps us answer common questions about how the church's new counseling ministry relates to professional counselors.

First, your counseling ministry can help those whose struggle fits in all three circles on the Venn diagram. For some people, it will fill the primary or exclusive role of helping. For others, it will play a supportive role. It is not a matter of deciding which category is best for everyone. Allow each participant to decide, as they work through their curriculum, which approach is the best fit for their life struggle.

For example, you may have someone in an anxiety group because they're having panic attacks resulting from a pending foreclosure on their home. In addition to attending the group, they would likely be meeting with an attorney for guidance on the foreclosure process and a physician or psychiatrist for medication to manage the panic attacks. But another person in the same anxiety group may only be seeking help from this group. Both approaches are fine. Ultimately, the participant decides.

Second, your counseling ministry should develop a two-way relationship with professionals in your community. Professional counselors are always looking for groups that can provide (1) supportive care for their active clients, (2) aftercare for their graduating counselees, or (3) free care for individuals without the financial means to afford counseling. As you develop a good relationship with the professional counselors in your community, you are likely to get as many referrals from them as you recommend to them.

As we will detail in chapter 17, building good relationships with these area professionals is an important way to get advisement on crisis situations and hard cases that emerge in your counseling ministry. Valuing a bidirectional relationship with area professionals reassures church leadership and concerned members that crisis situations will be handled well.

Third, your counseling ministry will focus primarily on shaping character through biblical instruction and navigating meaning of life challenges within a gospel paradigm.[1] These are the dominant approaches of ministry-based care. Understanding that people are embodied souls, where our bodies influence our souls as much as our souls influence our bodies, gives us the categories we need to recommend professionals when mental illness is a contributing factor to someone's life challenges. When participants in your ministry are also seeking professional counseling, the work done in your ministry will help them rightly interpret the benefits they receive from this care in light of their Christian faith.

---

1. To learn more about using these approaches in counseling, see the article "The Pastor as Counselor Lesson 6: Four Types of Counsel" at bradhambrick.com/pastorascounselor6/.

Section Two:
Three Spectrums
of Counseling Ethics
in Church-Based Care

Section one overviewed the foundational concepts and infrastructure necessary for starting a counseling ministry in your church. In section one, you learned that true counseling relationships are different from friendships. Both counseling and friendship are good, neither is better, but they are simply different. In section two, you will learn how to honor the ethical implications of these differences. If you are going to have a counseling ministry, you need to know how conduct these more formal relationships with integrity.

Chapter 13

INTRODUCING THE SPECTRUM
OF FORMALITY

Recall the picture of the dimly lit sitting room with the expensive vase of liability and the parallel between money designated for the church's building fund and information disclosed in counseling. We discussed the challenge these two comparisons represent—namely, the lack of clarity most churches have about how to handle the privileged information a counseling ministry receives—but we didn't resolve them.

In the next three chapters, we will begin to define how the rules of engagement change as a church moves from offering exclusively one-another care to having a counseling ministry. We will do this by defining three markers of a "more than friendship" relationship across three spectrums: formality, expertise, and jurisdiction. If you're not sure you know what those terms mean, don't worry—you will when we're finished.

In our examination of these three concepts, we will take each spectrum a couple of steps beyond what G4 and GCM are designed to provide, just as we did in our discussion of the five levels of competence (chapter 9). Don't let this overwhelm or intimidate you. Knowing what is beyond the scope of these ministries helps ensure that you can recognize when you're going beyond what your ministry is designed to do.

Our goal in these chapters is twofold. I want to

- define the markers that indicate that a change in relationship has occurred, and
- articulate what the resulting changes in the rules of engagement should be.

The clearer these markers are in your mind, the less awkward you will feel as you walk out their implications. The first-time leaders in your counseling ministry are taking on a "more than friendship" role and it is likely to feel weird, not because it's bad, but simply because it's new.

It's also important for the pastors in the church to have a firm grasp of these markers. The more your church leadership understands these differences, the more they can support your counseling ministry's operating according to wise ethical guidelines.

If you don't want the relationship changes discussed in these three chapters to occur, now is the time to realize you may not want a counseling ministry. That reveals that you only want to enrich the one-another ministry of your church. That's great too! If that is your goal, these chapters will help you stay within the confines of friendship ministry.

FORMALITY

To understand formality, let's start by defining an informal relationship. For our purposes, *informal* means a relationship in which anything moral and honoring is permissible. As long as you're not slandering, gossiping, or being rude, you're fine. How you relate to your friends, family, and coworkers—excluding anything that would necessitate repentance—is an example of informal relationship.

As you begin to think about relationships that are more formal than friendship, consider how you relate to your boss, a doctor, the clerk at a retail store, a government official, a speaker at a conference, etc. How would you articulate what is different in these relationships? What are the (largely unspoken) changes in the rules of engagement?

We'll use a spectrum (illustrated below) to give an overview of the changes that occur as we move from less formal relationships to more formal relationships. Here's how to interpret the line you will see, as well as those in the next two chapters:

Everything to the **left of the G4 and GCM emblems** represents the *types of care that belong to your church's one-another level (i.e., friendship) ministry.* Having a counseling ministry should not decrease the quality, depth, or emphasis these relationships receive in your church. Friendship should always be the majority care ministry of your church.

The **G4 and GCM emblems** represent *what your counseling ministry is and is not designed to do.* Your counseling ministry cannot be whatever people want it to be and be run well. You need to understand what the ministry does and does not do and be able to communicate that clearly.

Everything to the **right of the G4 and GCM emblems** represents *what is beyond the scope of your counseling ministry.* We need to know where the "do not cross lines" are so that good intentions don't take us into unwise liability.

Spectrum of Formality

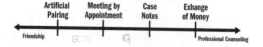

ESTABLISHING THE BASELINE OF FRIENDSHIP

Let's begin by asking, What do the parameters of friendship look like? This is an awkward question. Friends don't generally articulate the parameters of their relationship. Friendships don't have informed consent. We are defining the parameters here, not because this should be done in real life, but because we need to differentiate friendship from more formal helping relationships. Here are some markers of friendship:

- Friends hang out at whatever time fits both of their schedules.
- Friends exchange phone numbers and email addresses.
- Friends gauge the depth of what they share by the closeness of their friendship.
- It is not unusual for one friend to meet another's friends or family members.
- Either friend can initiate meeting with the other.
- In healthy friendship, the level of disclosure by both friends is relatively equal.

This level of formality (or lack thereof), should feel normal. It is what you experience with people in your small group, those on a ministry team with you at church, coworkers, classmates, people you know from the gym, etc. Reading this book should not change anything about those relationships. If you want to enhance the redemptive influence of these relationships throughout your church, consider reading *Transformative Friendships*.

I want to emphasize that counseling relationships aren't better than friendships. We're not trying to promote friendships into counseling relationships. We're not *ranking* which is better; we're *defining* what your church's counseling ministry offers so that you will recognize when the rules change.

THRESHOLD ONE: ARTIFICIAL PAIRING

This is the first threshold we cross. Friendships just happen. Usually there is no matchmaking process. When we form an artificially paired relationship, we begin to have role definition—a *helpee* seeking out a *helper*. The helpee comes to the helper for the purpose of overcoming a struggle or navigating a life transition. This is, therefore, a *goal-directed relationship*, and it is likely to discontinue when the goal is achieved.

Friendship exists on the left side of this first threshold; both G4 and GCM exist on the other side. Both ministries entail a church pairing someone requesting help with a group or mentor. The resulting relationship will exist as "more than friends" from its inception.

What are the implications of this?

Within the context of these more clearly defined roles, the helpee will be making vulnerable disclosures. Such disclosures are called *privileged information*, which is information received because of a formal helping role. If a friend shares information that was confided to them privately, it's called gossip. But if the helper in a more formal relationship shares privileged information (without permission), that is a breach of confidentiality. Both are morally wrong, but the latter also crosses into the domain of liability.

In moderately formal relationships, like those in G4 or GCM, if a participant wants their leader to share privileged information with an outside party, a simple email from the helpee granting permission to do so is adequate. Highly formal relationships (beyond what this book equips you to create) require a technical contract known as a Release of Information.

An example illustrates how permission works in the kind of counseling ministry we're discussing. GCM premarital mentors could say to their engaged couple, "We would love to be able to update the pastor officiating your wedding on our conversations. Do you mind connecting us via email?" Or in the case of a pastor reaching out to a G4 leader wanting an update on a group participant, the G4 leader should reply, "You would need to ask the participant to let me know if it is okay to answer your questions. If they send me an email giving that permission, I would be happy to talk."

THRESHOLD TWO: APPOINTED MEETING TIME

As we move beyond the second threshold—appointed meeting times—you will notice that GCM and G4 are on different sides of the line. GCM mentors are committing themselves to more "any-time" access to their mentees than a G4 leader is committing to group members.

Why is this? At least two factors are in play. First, GCM is most commonly used for mentoring engaged couples, which is usually less emotionally weighty than leading a G4 group. Therefore, the relationship can maintain more qualities of a friendship. If your church chooses to use GCM for postmarital mentoring,[1] it is recommended that you provide more structure to protect the emotional bandwidth of your mentors because those seeking postmarital care usually bring weightier struggles into helping conversations.

This again highlights the issue of sustainability for churches starting a counseling ministry. You must think of the care and longevity of the *helpers* you train, not just the care of the *helpees*. You have a shepherding responsibility for both. If the ministry is designed in a way that results in a high burnout rate for helpers, you will create situations in which helpees are abandoned in the middle of their course of care.

Second, the logistics of a group require meeting at a set time. This becomes an advantage as participants in group-based counseling benefit from learning about other participants' journeys. For this reason it is accurate to view a G4 leader as a choir conductor, who orchestrates the group, rather than as an instrument repairman, who cares for each individual. Knowing the unique benefits your ministry provides and the type of relationship it creates allows you to speak with clarity and confidence about what it does and doesn't do.

THRESHOLD THREE: TAKING CASE NOTES

Now we are crossing the threshold of writing case notes—a threshold you are discouraged from crossing with G4 or GCM, not because it is bad to take notes, but because churches are generally ill-equipped to navigate the unfamiliar terrain on the other side of this line.

After threshold one—artificial pairing—we noted that the helpee begins to become increasingly vulnerable with what they share. However, after threshold one, this information only resides in the mind of the helper. If you cross threshold three, that information lives on paper and abides in a file. If you cross threshold three, your church must know how to handle this recorded history properly.

---

1. At The Summit Church, we do not artificially pair post-marital mentors. We encourage small groups to study the GCM seminars together and forge naturally paired relationships for enriching their marriages.

A church's liability increases when it keeps detailed records of people's emotional and relational histories. The greater the significance of the privileged information a church stores, the greater the responsibility a church has to handle that information properly. Unless you have an experienced level-four counselor on staff (see chapter 9), it is not recommended that you cross this threshold. Once you begin to use case notes, you are launching a *counseling center* rather starting a *counseling ministry*.

THRESHOLD FOUR: FINANCIAL COMPENSATION

You are also discouraged from crossing the threshold of financial compensation in a church-based ministry. While there is nothing wrong with being paid to provide counseling, charging fees takes your ministry out from under the protection that Good Samaritan laws provide. These are laws that encourage those near a person in distress to assist that person without fear of liability. Also, when money is exchanged, both state licensing boards and the Internal Revenue Service begin to have some jurisdiction over your church's counseling ministry. (The extent of this jurisdiction varies based on state and financial arrangement. Guidance on this issue lies beyond the scope of this book.)

G4 and GCM are exclusively lay ministries, not professional models of counseling. Therefore, the lay leaders in these ministries are not compensated for their work. It is possible for a level-two counseling ministry to become large enough to warrant a church staff position to oversee and further develop it. If the content of this book were to lead to a vocational opportunity, it would be a salaried position for a ministry director, not a compensation-for-service arrangement with those receiving care. The lay leaders of G4 and GCM will always be lay volunteers, and the help they provide will always be free.

SUMMARIZING OUR JOURNEY

As we wrap up our discussion of the formality spectrum and look ahead to the expertise and jurisdiction spectrums, it makes sense to consider the question, How do these three spectrums relate to one another?

The image I would offer is that of an abacus. You may remember playing with one as a child. It had several tiers of rods with beads that slid across each rod. Imagine an abacus where each rod is a spectrum. The way an abacus works portrays how each spectrum is independent of the other two, but the three work together to appropriately define a helping relationship. For example, a ministry could be high formality, moderate expertise, and low jurisdiction.

Your responsibility is to know the combination and implications for any helping relationship your church creates. As we continue, you will see where G4 and GCM fall on each spectrum, so you'll know the implications for these ministries.

Chapter 14

INTRODUCING THE SPECTRUM
OF EXPERTISE

Now we begin our second journey from normal everyday relationships across a few thresholds toward care that is professional in nature. Remember, we are saying that a counselor can honor Jesus at every point across each spectrum. Our goal is to ensure that the helpers in our ministries know where their relationships are on each spectrum, so they know what honoring Christ and each counselee looks like in their role.

If our baseline concept for the spectrum of formality was friendship, our baseline concept for this chapter is respect. How much weight do we give to what someone says? The reality is, some people's words carry a lot of weight, and other people's words carry less. There are various reasons why we give more weight to some people's words, but one reason is that they may have special expertise in the matter at hand.

Consider this as you read this chapter: How much weight are we, as a church, asking participants in our counseling ministry to give to the words of their leaders and mentors? Another way of saying this is, How much of an *expert* are we claiming our G4 and GCM leaders are? You need to be clear on this before your pastor starts making Sunday morning announcements about the new ministry.

Don't get distracted here by the idea of giving weight to *their words*, as if it was the same as giving weight to *the Word*. While we want the words of our lay counselors to be rooted in the Word of the Wonderful Counselor (Isaiah 9:6), we need to recognize the differences between these two. When we take the timeless truths of the Bible and make timely applications to the details of an individual's life, we are necessarily making interpretations and inferences; this means that we should offer our advice humbly.[1]

Spectrum of Expertise

ESTABLISHING THE BASELINE OF RESPECT

If you were looking to buy a house, whose guidance would you value (i.e., respect) most? That of a realtor. But would you give the same weight to the realtor's counsel on the best schooling option for your children, the rash that showed up on your ankle, navigating conflict with your boss, a theological difference with a friend from small group, or your struggle with depression? Clearly not.

The point of these questions is to illustrate that we can give great weight to someone's opinion in one area of life without giving their opinion the same weight in every area of our lives. This is almost so obvious that it doesn't need to be said. But when a church launches a counseling ministry, it becomes a highly relevant point. To help us determine the extent to which we want participants to view our lay counseling ministry leaders as experts, let's consider five different areas of life in which respect can be given to people.

1. I respect your *character*. I think you make godly choices.
2. I respect your *integrity*. I think you will follow through on what you say.

---

1. For more guidance on how to interpret the Bible for the ministry of counseling, I recommend Michael Emlet's book *Cross Talk: Where Life and Scripture Meet* (Greensboro, NC: New Growth Press, 2009).

3. I respect your *performance*. I think you are excellent at what you do.

4. I respect your *opinions*. I think you ask good questions and arrive at fair conclusions.

5. I respect your *counsel*. I think you know my situation well and how to resolve it.

The first two points (regarding character and integrity) mention prerequisites for serving in any church ministry. But while the absence of these qualities disqualifies someone from serving in your counseling ministry, the presence of these qualities alone doesn't make someone a good lay counselor. We need to be honest enough to admit that there are some sweet, sincere, God-fearing people in our churches who aren't great at managing their own lives (performance) or who impose their own experiences onto other people's stories (opinions), and thus for these reasons wouldn't be good at giving emotional–relational guidance (counsel).

The third point (performance) is what catches the most attention in a social setting, and churches are social environments. We notice whether people are successes in business, good athletes, effective communicators, etc. But performance in these areas has next to nothing to do with someone being qualified to serve in a counseling ministry. This point is the equivalent of acknowledging that just because someone makes an A in math doesn't mean they're good at interpreting poetry.

The fourth point (about asking good questions and arriving at fair conclusions) is an important skill for a counselor. If someone frames questions in a one-sided way or shows a high degree of bias in their conclusions, they will not be an effective counselor. But this skill, while vitally important, still doesn't get at the variable of expertise we are considering in this chapter.

The fifth point (ability to give good counsel) is what we want to be able to communicate effectively when we describe the leaders in our lay counseling ministries. This is what determines how much weight a church is asking participants to give to the words of those who lead in G4 and GCM.

Let's look now at the spectrum that measures this quality—the spectrum of counseling expertise. The three thresholds we'll examine represent the levels of preparation or training the helper is expected to have.

THRESHOLD ONE: PERSONAL EXPERIENCE

Threshold one is the "knowing what it's like" level of expertise, because they have "been there." If you read Hebrews 2:17 and 4:14–16, you can't help but notice how important this experiential type of knowledge is. The Bible says we can pray with confidence because we know that Jesus understands what we're going through. Communication is easier and richer when someone has experienced something comparable to our hardship.

Personal experience is the only type of expertise a G4 or GCM leader is asked to bring. The curriculum contains categories of assessment and strategies for change. Each G4 and GCM leader uses their personal experience as one testimony of what it looks like to take the journey mapped by the curriculum.

This means that premarital mentors bring the personal experience of having been married and cultivating a healthy home life. It means that G4 leaders for addiction, eating disorders, or trauma groups have lived with these experiences. The mentee or group participant knows that their leader has life experience with what they're facing.

Notice we say that the leader's personal experience is *one* testimony of the change process. The leader's testimony isn't *the* example everyone in the group should follow, but it is *one* example. The curriculum is the map, and a leader's testimony narrates one person's journey across that terrain.

This point is important for volunteer recruitment. Many viable mentors and group leaders will be intimidated out of leading if they feel like being a lay counselor requires them to be an expert. Most of us know that having a testimony doesn't make us an expert. But when a potential leader realizes that their role is to facilitate a structured process and provide encouragement along the way, it seems both achievable and enjoyable.

A personal experience level of expertise communicates, "This journey is possible. There is hope." Hope is the variable that correlates with successful counseling as much as any other element. The value of knowing someone who has weathered the challenge you are facing is hard to overestimate. It is a resource that is abundantly available in our local churches. Ministries like G4 and GCM help us harvest more of the ministry potential that exists in our churches.

THRESHOLD TWO: CERTIFICATION LEVEL TRAINING

Threshold two—where counselors have some form of lay certification—takes us into the muddy middle again. A variety of certification programs train lay counselors. What these have in common is equipping laypeople to serve as *general practitioners* of counseling; that is, as counselors who meet with an individual or couple, triage primary needs, develop counseling goals, take case notes, create a treatment plan, and oversee the change process. Hopefully, you are seeing clearly how this is beyond the scope of G4 and GCM.

When a church platforms lay counselors in this role of general practitioners of counseling, it is hard not to give the impression that these lay counselors have more expertise than the certification process actually provides. Therefore it is easy for a helpee to assume that their helper is a professional counselor volunteering their time. When this happens, the counselee gives more weight to the counselor's words than their expertise warrants.

This problem can be prevented by having intake forms with a well-worded informed consent section describing the counselor's training and differentiating this training from that of a licensed counselor. But even when accurate informed consent is provided, this counseling model still asks the layperson to perform many of the functions of a professional counselor with much less training.

Contrasting what would be expected of lay counselors who cross this second threshold with what is expected of a G4 leader or GCM mentor should bring further clarity about these group ministries. In G4 and GCM, a lay leader is asked to be good at caring for only one need—the need they have personal experience with and is the topic of the curriculum they are facilitating. Meanwhile, after threshold two, a lay counselor is expected to provide care for a wide variety of needs and create an individualized treatment plan for each person they counsel.

THRESHOLD THREE: ADVANCED EDUCATION

At this level, the counselor has completed at least a master's degree in counseling and is usually licensed (LPC, LMHC, LMFT, or LCSW). If your ministry begins utilizing someone with this level of qualification, you are creating a counseling center that is best operated alongside your church, rather than as a counseling ministry in your church.

Nonprofit counseling centers that promote and structure themselves to offer distinctively Christian care are wonderful. But these are separate organizations, rather than ministries of a local church. They require a financially self-sustaining business model and are not operated by volunteers.

SUMMARY

In a G4 and GCM model of ministry, lay leaders have a *personal experience level of expertise*. They use their life experience as a testimony as they guide group members through a structured curriculum. This approach increases the number of people willing to serve voluntarily in a counseling ministry. The clarity regarding the training and role of these leaders gives participants an accurate picture—and accurate expectations—of the care provided, thereby reducing the liability concerns for the church.

Chapter 15

INTRODUCING THE SPECTRUM
OF JURISDICTION

By now you know the drill: we describe a concept, define a few thresholds, and point out where G4 and GCM fit on the spectrum. Don't allow the predictable rhythm of these chapters to distract you from assimilating the content because, of the three spectrums we are considering, jurisdiction is the most complex, and the lines are the least clear-cut.

The concepts for the jurisdiction spectrum are *influence* and *authority*. You start a counseling ministry because you want to be a positive influence in the lives of people who are hurting. You want to help people change in ways that will help them flourish.

In this chapter, we're trying to find the line for what we can do and what we shouldn't do when someone needs to change but doesn't want to. We don't want to use the relational influence of counseling to coerce change, and to avoid doing that we need to find the line between positive influence and hurtful coercion. We want to avoid infusing counseling influence with the church's authority in a way that is harmful for participants and creates liability for the church.

That line is not as simple and clear as we would like. What about the husband/father who refuses to admit his addiction and makes his family's life erratic? What about the wife/mother whose anxiety is becoming compulsive and is paralyzing her family? How much and what type of influence should the church assert? How much of that influence should be asserted by the church's counseling ministry? These are the kind of questions we are grappling with in this chapter.

Let's use a parallel example. We will oversimplify it for the purpose of this illustration. Some people at your church may think your lay counselors should have the same level of influence as a social worker at child protective services (CPS). What does that mean? Social workers at CPS have more jurisdictional authority than other counselors. Their influence extends to the authority of imposing consequences. If parents are not providing a safe living environment for their children because of abuse or neglect, these social workers have the authority, under the state, to remove children from the home.

Comparably, some Christians want the counseling ministry to enforce consequences, under the authority of the church, on counselees who are not following the example of Christ. They reason that there should be some way to *make* somebody change who doesn't want to change. The force of the verb *make* reveals that they have an unhealthy understanding of the role of influence in counseling.

The counseling ministry of a church cannot make people change. Counseling is a place of *voluntary participation* and *voluntary change*. On an occasion when church discipline is needed—involving the jurisdictional authority of a church—this is led by the church pastors. Church discipline is not a function of the counseling ministry. At most, the counseling ministry serves as a consultant to the pastors, with the participant's permission.

There's a tension here that's unique to counseling in the context of the church. A church is a character-based membership organization. People join a church by embracing the gospel and committing to live a Christlike life. (This is not a complete picture of the church, of course, but this limited description helps us get at the confusion that lies at the intersection of jurisdiction and church-based counseling.) Like any membership organization, a church has the right to remove from membership those who live at odds with its ideals and mission. But most membership organizations do not have counseling entities embedded within them. Given this situation, some tension and confusion are inevitable.

Let's look at the spectrum of jurisdiction. As we move across it, we will wrestle with the question, What does it mean for a membership organization to have a counseling entity within it?

Spectrum of Jurisdiction

ESTABLISHING THE BASELINE OF INFLUENCE

At its basic level, *influence* is the capacity to affect someone's choices, beliefs, or values. In practice, influence is usually domain-specific: a boss has influence over how we do our jobs, a teacher has influence over class assignments, and a coach has influence over roles on the team.

These examples help us further clarify the aspect of influence we are discussing in this chapter. How much and what type of influence does a church have, and how much—if any—of that influence does its counseling ministry possess? Ultimately, of course, the leadership of a church has authority ("final say" influence) to oversee the membership process of that church. However, because most of a church's care happens in the context of friendships, most of a church's influence lies in peer relationships.

Peer influence is the baseline for our spectrum of jurisdiction.

Peer relationships have *influence without authority*. There is no hierarchy or role definition in friendship; there is mutual influence. As soon as one friend becomes the "makes good choices and keeps me out of trouble" friend, the friendship evolves (or devolves) into a helping relationship. Influence is no longer mutual and balanced; the relationship is becoming one-sided. This dynamic has ruined many friendships and burned out many responsible friends.

You may hear the phrase "influence without authority" and think, *What about accountability partners?* After all, this type of peer-based relationship is common in churches. When we have an accountability partner, we give them *permission* to ask what would otherwise be intrusive questions. But permission to ask is not authority to impose consequences. When we discuss jurisdiction, we are talking about more than mutually agreed upon social influence.

It may be helpful to consider the different ways that peer-level relationships have unauthoritative influence, meaning no one forces or coerces the other into making changes they do not voluntarily embrace. Peers influence each other in the following ways:

- *Example*—One way we explore our world is by observing the choices of our friends. We discover what works and what doesn't via their choices.
- *Compelling personality*—Our friends respond to the world differently than we do. Extroverts enjoy relationships in a way that is contagious. Introverts display the value of careful reflection in a way that displays its benefits. Having friends who are different from us changes us.
- *Opportunity to try new things*—Every time a friend says, "Do you want to do [this activity]?," it is an invitation to expand our horizons. The varying interests of our friends shape us.
- *Alternative perspectives*—Each time a friend replies, "Really? I'm not sure I see it that way," they inadvertently chip away at our self-centeredness.
- *Embodying values*—Integrity, loyalty, and other values are just concepts until we see them in practice. Relationships make values three-dimensional and breathe life into definitions. Being blessed by the Christlike character of a friend inspires us to be that kind of person.

All relationships have these types of influence. We want these types of influence to be used within the friendships of our churches to compel all of us toward greater Christlikeness. Without this type of body-life influence within a church, sermons and Bible studies become too much like academic lectures, cut off from the realities of everyday life.

With this understanding of peer influence as our foundation, we are going to turn our attention to answering the main questions of this chapter: What types of "more than friends" influence can occur within the counseling ministry of a membership organization? And how do we steward this influence in a way that honors the person receiving care?

THRESHOLD ONE: ROLE INFLUENCE

We observed above that there is no definition of roles in friendships between peers and that influence is mutual. In crossing the first threshold, that changes. When the people involved in a relationship take on specified roles, the person in the leadership role has greater influence than they would have had in a peer friendship. Both G4 and GCM cross this threshold. In GCM, leaders are called mentors, and in G4, leaders are called facilitators, but regardless of the title, by virtue of being the leader, these individuals have additional influence.

As a group facilitator, the G4 leader expresses influence by guiding the discussion, drawing out participants who are reticent to speak, curtailing participants who don't know when to stop talking, identifying unhealthy dynamics that emerge in the group, and keeping up with where people are in their journey through the curriculum.[1] Even the reality that new guests to G4 naturally turn to the leader for clarification when something is unclear shows a pivotal position of influence.

Mentors in GCM express influence by taking the lead in scheduling meetings, drawing from a longer history of being married, choosing to share only those parts of their personal history that serve their mentees, and having the freedom to raise yellow flag or red flag concerns that emerge about the mentee couple's relationship.

---

1. The training to equip G4 leaders to effectively fulfill these roles is provided in *Facilitating*.

However, the influence G4 and GCM leaders have is leadership without authority. They are guiding the process, answering questions, and offering advice, but they have no standing to enforce anything they recommend. This sphere of "leadership without authority" is where almost all counseling—secular or Christian, licensed or lay—exists. *Counselors don't tell anyone what to do.* They make suggestions (hopefully well-informed, biblically based suggestions), but it's up to the counselees to decide whether to follow them.

In discussing this lack of authority we again bump up against something that makes many Christians uncomfortable. "Doesn't the Bible have authority?" we might ask. Yes, it does. It declares what God deems right and good. At the final judgment, the standards revealed in the Bible will be the measure by which our lives are evaluated (2 Corinthians 5:10). But the Bible having authority over morality is not the same thing as a counselor having authority over a counselee. Counselors can faithfully point people to God's standard, but they can't force them to adhere to it or punish them if they do not.

THRESHOLD TWO: MEMBERSHIP INFLUENCE

If you felt like that last paragraph was incomplete, as if it did not represent the totality of a church's ministry, you were correct. A counseling ministry does not embody the totality of the church's ministry. It does one part. Hopefully, it does that part well. But a counseling ministry should be able to recognize when a participant's situation has crossed into another domain.

At the end of the previous section, we should want to say, "But there are times when *a church* [not a counseling ministry] must uphold God's standard by removing from membership someone who willfully rejects God's standard." That brings us to threshold number two: membership influence.

Membership influence is "in or out" authority. Does someone belong to the membership organization or not? The pastors lead a church in exercising this type of authority, and if a concern emerges that is believed to warrant disfellowshiping, that authority is shared by the church as a whole.

But just because G4 and GCM do not themselves have membership influence, that does not mean G4 and GCM will be uninvolved. You need to understand how the leaders in your counseling ministry should and shouldn't interact with pastoral leadership when a church needs to exert membership authority.

First, remember that what participants share in the context of the counseling ministry is privileged information. This means that leaders in your counseling ministry should have a participant's permission before sharing their information. The only exception to this is when there is a legal requirement to breach confidentiality (see the next threshold).

When a participant shares information about their life with a G4 or GCM leader, they are not agreeing to share that information with the pastoral staff. For this reason, if a pastor or elder asks for an update on someone in the counseling ministry, the answer should be, "I would be happy to talk with you, but you [the pastor] need to ask them [the participant] to send me an email giving me permission." If the participant does not give permission, then the church leaders must proceed based on the information the individual is willing to give them access to.[2]

Another question that frequently emerges is whether disclosure of a significant sin pattern to the church's counseling ministry should initiate the counseling ministry sharing that information with a pastor. The answer is no. If someone is reaching out for help, they are not showing a hard-hearted disposition toward their sin. If pastoral care is needed in addition to counseling (see chapter 10 for more on this distinction), the individual should be encouraged to talk with a pastor, and the G4 or GCM leader should offer to support the participant in this process.

There is one more caveat in this threshold: *At least 50 percent of what is discussed in your counseling ministry will be suffering-focused, not sin-focused.* (I'm using the figure 50 percent to illustrate that life

---

2. For a restorative church discipline process that seeks to work cooperatively with counseling (both inside and outside the church) and honor constraints on privileged information, see bradhambrick.com/churchdiscipline.

struggles come from two sources—sin and suffering, the effects of our fallen nature and the effects of living in a fallen world. The number 50 percent is not a precise measure or an ideal to aspire to in your ministry.) Therefore, this discussion of church discipline should not cause us to conclude that everything discussed in counseling is sin-focused. That assumption causes Christians to be hesitant about seeking care for suffering-based struggles.

THRESHOLD THREE: PUNITIVE INFLUENCE

We've discussed how counseling ministries like G4 and GCM relate to the church. Now we turn to the relationship between the church and the governing authorities.

The government has established laws that govern when privileged information is protected (that is, when it falls under *pastor-parishioner privilege* and should not be shared) and when it must, by law, be passed on to the authorities. A church needs to understand what types of disclosures fall under mandated reporting requirements. Typically, these involve abuse or neglect of children or the elderly and threats of immediate harm to oneself or others. Honoring these reporting requirements is a clear implication of what it means to obey Romans 13.[3]

The church does not have the jurisdictional authority to usurp the civil rights of individuals in ways that abuse situations require. For example, if the church tried to remove a child from a dangerous home against the parent's wishes, this would be kidnapping. However, child protective services (CPS) does have the jurisdictional authority to do this when it needs to be done.

This does not mean the church has no role in situations where civil authorities are involved. The church has many roles it should fulfill in such cases. Families in situations where abuse is occurring need more than a social worker and police officer. They need friends, benevolence, logistical assistance, encouragement, spiritual guidance, etc. But they also need a social worker and police officer.

---

3. For an overview of how to respond to child abuse, as well as other forms of abuse that do not fall under mandated reporting requirements, see the curriculum *Becoming a Church that Cares Well for the Abused* (www.churchcares.com).

As we discussed in chapter 11, having a counseling ministry will get your church involved in more situations where multiple jurisdictions are active. The church's role in multi-jurisdiction situations is to provide supportive relational influence (friendship and pastoral care) and to discipline unruly members (threshold two), while being supportive of the governing authorities (threshold three). Having a clear understanding of this role is vital to navigating these situations well.

You could summarize the three thresholds of influence and authority discussed in this chapter in three points:

1. *Role influence* exists in both G4 and GCM and results in privileged information.
2. *Membership influence* belongs to the church, not the counseling ministry.
3. *Punitive influence* belongs to the governing authorities (Romans 13:1–6), not the church.

CONCLUSION

As you are now concluding section two, you should understand and be able to explain where GCM and G4 fall on spectrums of formality, expertise, and jurisdiction. These terms should mean more to you than they did three chapters ago. Your ability to articulate what makes G4 and GCM "more than friendship but less than professional counseling" is what ensures participants understand the type of care these ministries provide and, thereby, protects your church from avoidable liability.

Section Three:
How Would We Start
a Counseling Ministry?

Section three is what you were looking for when you began reading this book. You wanted to know how to start a counseling ministry. Now that you understand the infrastructure and ethics of overseeing a church-based counseling ministry, you are ready to begin thinking through a launch plan. That is what we will look at in section three.

Chapter 16

AN INTENTIONAL SIX-PHASE APPROACH
TO LAUNCHING G4 OR GCM

In this chapter, you'll be converting the many concepts you've been learning about into concrete plans. We have a lot of nuts and bolts to cover, but if you've been excited about the possibilities we've explored to this point, it will be worth it as you see how a real, live counseling ministry takes shape!

If you are preparing to launch GCM, the process is straightforward. GCM seeks to do one thing well as a formal ministry: premarital mentoring. As we've discussed, the GCM curriculum can also be used as a small group study, but that falls under the church's general discipleship ministry; it is not part of a counseling ministry, so it won't appear as part of this launch plan.

If you are preparing to launch G4, you are approaching this chapter from one of two places. Either you are in the early stages of a major new ministry initiative at your church, or you are coalescing numerous, independent G4 groups into a cohesive ministry. This chapter is written primarily from the perspective that you are preparing for a large-scale launch of a G4 or GCM at your church.

If you are coalescing existing G4 groups, be encouraged—you'll feel like you're ahead of the game. Your focus will be on how to effectively centralize a ministry that began decentralized. Making this transition well is as important as starting from scratch well. You want to honor the work volunteers have already been doing by communicating clearly throughout this process.

Whatever lies ahead for you—starting a premarital GCM mentorship program, launching a new G4 ministry, or consolidating already-existing G4 groups—we will cover the following six phases:

1. Identify leaders and curriculum
2. Clarify key aspects of informed consent
3. Ensure lay leaders understand roles and referrals
4. Secure a consultation relationship
5. Carry out ministry as designed
6. Add additional ministries through the same process

PHASE ONE: IDENTIFY LEADERS AND CURRICULUM

This is a classic ministry chicken or egg question: which comes first—good leaders or good programs? Both are necessary. In terms of order of operation, either can come first. But when it comes to which most impacts the success of a ministry, there is no question—*no ministry will be more effective than the quality of its leaders.* Curriculum is important, but leaders are essential.

What does this mean? Don't launch a ministry just because you are excited about a curriculum. Let the people of your church—their life experiences, skills, and needs—determine what you implement. Remember our guiding principle for a lay counseling ministry: *Do what your church can do well and grow steadily from there.*

Does that mean that finding a leader always comes chronologically before identifying a curriculum? No. It does mean that when we get excited about a curriculum, we need to be careful not to allow our enthusiasm to rush the vetting and training of leaders. When ill-prepared or immature leaders are given leadership roles in a counseling ministry, their involvement is inevitably short-lived. And when this happens, the participants suffer most.

Considering this, phase one can be completed in one of two ways.

1. You are approached by a potential leader with an area of passion (addiction, trauma, blended families, premarital preparation, etc.) and find a curriculum that meets this need well.

2. You find a curriculum that addresses a need in your congregation or community and recruit leaders who can facilitate that curriculum well.

Even after you have an established counseling ministry, both paths will remain active. You will sometimes be approached by leaders and then need to find a curriculum. You may have a leader move away, so you'll need to identify a new leader for that group. Or you could have multiple people with a shared need approach you about a group, and then you try to identify both a leader and curriculum.

View this six-phase launch model as cyclical, realizing you will come back to phase one each time you expand your G4 offerings. This means you will perpetually need to be proficient in three sets of questions, two for G4 and one for GCM.

Finding a G4 facilitator

The following are questions for vetting a potential G4 facilitator:

- Does this person show evidence that they understand and have embraced the gospel?
- Can they talk about their life experiences or struggle without becoming brittle or overbearing?
- Do they have the social skills to manage a group grappling with difficult experiences?
- Have they shown the willingness to commit to a ministry role for an extended duration (at least twelve months are recommended)?
- Can they navigate the successes and failures of group members without taking either personally?

Too often, churches are prone to platform leaders because this opportunity will be good for a leader's growth. While that is fine in some settings, *in a counseling ministry, you only platform leaders who are ready to facilitate the growth of others*. Leaders who are not ready to fill their counseling role will inadvertently but inevitably hurt the participants in that ministry. A counseling ministry exists to care for the participants, not to provide a growth experience for the leader.

When leaders abandon a role because it's emotionally overwhelming, they personalize the ups and downs of participants, or they are unreliable due to other commitments, they hurt those under their care. As part of a church starting a counseling ministry, you have an obligation to screen for these concerns before you allow an individual to lead.

Finding a G4 curriculum

The following are questions for vetting a potential new curriculum for G4:[1]

- Does the curriculum have a holistic rather than anecdotal or testimonial take on its subject—that is, is it a well-rounded curriculum that reflects the many experiences people can have as they work through their struggle, or does it focus on a narrow range of experiences that not everyone will be able to relate to?
- Does the curriculum have a distinctively Christian perspective?
- Is the curriculum more of a discipleship course that should be a small group study instead of a G4 curriculum?

A good group curriculum can facilitate the journey of a variety of people who share the same struggle. For example, not every person struggling with addiction has the same motives or temptations. A highly anecdotal or testimonial resource will tend to be effective only for people whose stories or personalities happen to closely align with the author's. Testimonial books are wonderful for providing hope, but they do not make good G4 curriculum.

You also want each curriculum to have a counseling focus. For example, a Bible study on suffering from the book of Job would be

---

1. A list of possible curriculums is available at "24 Possible Curriculum for a G4 Ministry," bradhambrick.com/G4curriculum. In addition, chapter 15 of *Facilitating* contains further guidance on vetting and selecting curriculums that do not use the G4 nine-step models.

better suited for the church's discipleship ministry than G4, as would a Christian book on parenting. But a study on navigating the unique challenges of chronic pain or a blended family would be a good fit for G4. Think of the difference this way: *By attending G4, a participant is revealing more about themselves than the average person would be comfortable sharing in the general discipleship context.*

As you complete step one for a G4 ministry, you should be able to complete a chart like this one.

Leader Name	Subject Area	Curriculum Name	Leader Vetted	Curriculum Vetted
			Yes / No	Yes / No
			Yes / No	Yes / No
			Yes / No	Yes / No
			Yes / No	Yes / No
			Yes / No	Yes / No

Finding a GCM mentor couple

The following are questions for vetting a potential GCM mentor couple:

- Do both husband and wife give evidence that they understand and have embraced the gospel?
- Have they been married for at least five years? Your church may decide to increase the required number of years a couple needs to be married to mentor. But five years is the minimal amount of marriage experience recommended for a mentor couple.
- Are they actively caring for and deepening their marriage?
- Do they show the ability to offer perspective without imposing their preferences?
- Do they have a track record of sustaining long-term friendships?

A GCM ministry does one thing—premarital mentoring—but you will continually be vetting and training prospective mentors.

That means you will need to return to the questions above. However, the curriculum for GCM is set. That is why there is one set of questions for GCM instead of two, as there is for G4.

The value of mentoring is largely dependent on the duration of the relationship. The longer the mentoring relationship, the more benefit it has. Therefore, having a track record of sustaining friendships is a key indicator of whether a couple will be quality mentors. Ideally, mentoring relationships will endure informally for decades after the formal mentoring process is complete.

Another quality for good mentors is the ability to offer advice without imposing preferences. Good mentoring doesn't presume that what worked for us will work for you, so your marriage should look like our marriage. Good mentors get to know the engaged couples and help them cultivate a marriage culture that fits their unique personalities and aptitudes. The mentor couple's marriage is an example of how they try to honor God's design for marriage given their own personalities and aptitudes.

PHASE TWO: CLARIFY KEY ASPECTS OF INFORMED CONSENT

From the very beginning of launching your new ministry you want to do everything you can to reduce your church's liability. People in your church will understandably ask, "Are we going to get in trouble if something goes wrong in this new counseling ministry?" The answer to their question will be determined by how well you do three things. The Big Three points for liability reduction follow:

1. Obtain clear informed consent (covered here in phase two).
2. Ensure that leaders minister within their roles (covered next in phase three).
3. Utilize a ministry only as it is designed to be used (covered in phase five).

As you can see, informed consent is at the top of the list. The big idea of informed consent is that *every counselee—even if you call them a group participant or mentee—should always know what they're getting.* It is the church's responsibility to make sure this happens. To be effective, informed consent shouldn't be complicated. The information provided about the nature of the ministry should be clear and consistent, and it should answer these three basic questions:

- What is the training and role of the helper?
- What are the expectations and responsibilities of the helpee?
- What type of activities or disclosures are involved in this helping relationship?

In a ministry like G4, informed consent is not something you create for each new group. G4 only needs one informed consent form for all its groups. But if your church is launching GCM in addition to G4, you will need to create a separate informed consent.

The answers to the questions above should be available everywhere people can learn about or sign up for the ministry: the church website, promotional pieces, registration forms, etc. In ministries of moderate formality, like G4 and GCM, informed consent does not need to be worded like a contract the way it would be at a professional counseling center (where counselees read and sign a detailed policy review). Simple, conversational language posted at each stage of the ministry entry process is sufficient.

Flip back to the early parts of chapters 3 and 5. These definitions of G4 and GCM are informed consent statements. They describe what these ministries are, who the leaders are, and what the participants are expected to do.[2]

Participants commonly get inaccurate information when they call the church. In some churches, multiple people share phone-answering duties, and they won't all have an equally clear understanding of G4 and GCM. This can be a problem. Therefore, all questions about the counseling ministry should be directed to the same person. When this person is uncertain about the answer to a caller's question, they need to be comfortable saying, "I'm not sure. That's a good question. Let me ask, so I can make sure I give you accurate information. I will call you back as soon as I have the answer for you."

---

2. Additional examples of informed consent can be found at summitchurch.com/G4 and summitchurch.com/GCM.

PHASE THREE: ENSURE LAY LEADERS UNDERSTAND ROLES AND REFERRALS

Roles and referrals are two sides of the same coin. When a G4 or GCM leader knows the limits of their role, it invites the question, "What happens if someone needs care beyond what I do?" Without a clear answer to this question the lay leader will be prone to, with the best of intentions, go beyond what they are equipped to do.

Ensuring that helpers stay within the limits of their role is the second of the three points of liability reduction. Liability emerges when leaders do more than they were equipped to do or try to fulfill roles outside of those the participant was informed were part of the ministry.

You can and should help ensure that your lay leaders stay within their role by (a) having an established next-level referral list, and (b) role-playing during leader orientation situations where the lay leader should recommend another resource.

To create a next-level referral list, start by asking yourself, *If we start a ministry for [blank], what community contacts are we likely to need?* For example, if you start an addiction group, you need to know a detox center; if you start an eating disorder group, you need to know a nutritionist; if you start a group for anxiety and depression, you need to know a psychiatrist you can recommend.

As you call counseling resources in the community to build your referral list, expect to be received well. You are calling to offer them business. They should like that. Here is a basic outline you can reference to guide the conversation.

1. At our church, we are starting a GCM and/or G4 ministry for [subjects]. [Explain what that means.]
2. We appreciate your work with [struggle related to your ministry].
3. When someone needs care beyond what we provide, we want to be prepared to connect them with quality resources in our community.
4. How would you want us to describe your work to a participant in our ministry?

5. What types of care do you provide that would be relevant to those participating in G4 and/or GCM?

6. What is the best way for us to connect a potential new client with you?

7. Are there other professionals in our community you believe we should know about and connect with as we are starting this ministry?

Question 7 helps to make sure your next-level referral list is holistic. You don't have to know every resource you need to create a good referral list. You just need to make the first call and ask for additional guidance. When you stop getting new contacts, you have gotten to know the resources in your community. If you get an enthusiastic response about your church-based counseling ministry, consider asking one more question:

8. We have a regular training and encouragement time for our leaders. Would you be willing to come and help us equip our leaders?

You especially want to get to know the Christian counselors in your community. These individuals are invaluable. Phase four discusses other benefits that emerge as these relationships develop into a consultation arrangement, and chapter 17 has guidance on building a relationship with your referral contacts.

The decision to make a referral is not as self-evident or emotionally easy to navigate as it might seem. For this reason, role-playing these conversations should be part of your onboarding process for new leaders. Think through the stressful situations that would commonly come up in a group meeting or mentoring relationship. For example,

- Someone in the addiction group talks about "feeling like they're going to die" because of their withdrawal symptoms.
- Someone from the eating disorder group passes out at work or school.

- Someone from the depression group abruptly gets inordinately "happy" (suggesting a manic episode).
- One fiancé is pressuring the other not to be honest about their relationship for fear their mentors will discourage them from getting married.

Role-play these kinds of situations with your prospective G4 and GCM leaders, and play the part of the resistant participant. As you role-play, give opposition to what the G4 or GCM leader is suggesting, and try to pressure them to ignore or neglect the appropriate next step. That may look like one of these responses:

- Blow off the need to seek additional care.
- Demand that the leader do more than they're equipped to do (e.g., fix the problem privately).
- Spiritualize resisting additional care as an expression of faith and trusting God.
- Demean their unwillingness to offer more care as being unloving.

The first time your leaders try to navigate conversations like these shouldn't be with a ministry participant. Role-playing does more than give the new leader a practice run; it assures the leader that you will support them as they limit the scope of their care to what a group or mentoring ministry is designed to provide.

Chapter 17 of this book gives additional advice on when to refer participants for outside help, and appendix B of *Facilitating* ("What to Do When Something Goes Bad-Bad") gives group leaders more complete guidance on handling situations where a participant needs a referral for next-level help.

PHASE FOUR: SECURE A CONSULTATION RELATIONSHIP

Phase three raises a question that causes many churches to shy away from starting a counseling ministry: What will we do when we realize we are in over our heads? The answer is (or at least should be) consult with someone experienced in that level of crisis care.

The list you started making in phase two is where you find this person. As you survey professionals in your community, you want to find a Christian counselor who is excited about your new ministry. Their crisis management experience and awareness of the resources in your community are invaluable to your emerging ministry. A consultant needs to be a level-four counselor (see chapter 9) who has experience working with CPS, attorneys, psychiatrists, law enforcement, and other comparable professionals. A licensed counselor who has been in your community for several years will have this type of experience.

Consultation is likely the first consistent financial investment your church will make in the counseling ministry. Often, when a church considers an initial investment in counseling, they envision providing scholarships to see a local counselor. But this is not cost effective as a long-term strategy. Ten counseling sessions for a single individual or family can easily cost $1,000 if they don't have insurance. That is not a viable precedent for most churches to set.

For the same cost as one to two counseling sessions per month, a counselor can consult with you, the G4 and/or GCM director, on the hard situations that emerge in these ministries. Chapter 17 gives guidance for helping the consultant understand the ethical implications of and guidelines for their involvement in this role. By investing in a consultation relationship, the church is investing in their G4 and/ or GCM director's crises management education. Thus the church is getting both short-term (i.e., well-managed care for a crisis) and long-term benefit (i.e., an enriched leader) from their investment.

The conclusion to phase four involves inviting your consultant to review chapters 13–15 of this book and the plans you developed in phases one to three of this chapter. Chapters 13–15 will help the counselor orient themselves to the ethical guidelines for a lay counseling ministry. Reviewing phases one to three will let them know what your church is currently attempting to do so that they can help you identify blind spots in the planning process.

PHASE FIVE: CARRY OUT THE MINISTRY AS DESIGNED

This is the final of the Big Three points of liability reduction. Once you set the ministry up to succeed, stay within the confines of what you created. After all, that is the point of setting things up well. You put the effort in early so that once you launch the counseling ministry, your leaders can focus on the task at hand with peace of mind.

Phase five raises the question, When would we not carry out the ministry *as designed*? The most likely answer is during a crisis that most elicits your leaders' compassion. These are the moments when helpers begin to blend formal and informal styles of care; they change their mindset from that of a counseling leader with a defined role (level-two care, see chapter 9) to that of a friend willing to do whatever you need (level-one care). The care instinct is good, but the counseling outcome often is not.

A consistent theme with your G4 or GCM leaders should be that when a situation calls for something *more than* or *different from* what they've been prepared to offer, they need to consult with the director. Here are some examples of situations that might emerge:

- A G4 participant needs pastoral care and wants their G4 leader to fill this role. Instead, the group facilitator should help the participant identify the pastor best suited to care for this need, inform them how to contact this pastor, and offer to support the participant in the process of reaching out to the pastor for pastoral care.
- A GCM couple needs benevolence help and wants their mentors to serve as advocates to lobby the church for assistance. Instead, the mentors should inform the couple about how the church handles benevolence needs, whom to contact, and offer support to them as they reach out for help.
- A G4 participant in crisis wants their group facilitator to provide individualized counseling. Instead, the facilitator should help the participant connect with a counselor who can provide this individualized counsel by consulting with their

G4 director, giving the participant the counselor's contact information, and encouraging the participant to schedule an appointment.

- A G4 participant is dissatisfied that G4 isn't providing the sense of community they desire from the church. The G4 facilitator should affirm the desire for Christian community and use this as an opportunity to reinforce G4 Core Value 7, "transitions into the church's discipleship ministries," (see chapter 3 for a brief list of core values and chapter 4 of *Facilitating* for a more complete description of each). Then the facilitator should help the participant identify the contact person for the church's small group ministry.

You should notice the following pattern:

1. G4 and GCM do what G4 and GCM are designed to do.
2. When needs beyond what G4 and GCM address emerge, leaders
   a. affirm the validity of these needs,
   b. help the participant identify the relevant resource, and
   c. offer to support the participant in reaching out to this resource.
3. G4 and GCM continue doing what G4 and GCM are designed to do.

When each leader understands their role well enough to follow this pattern, a church can have a liability-wise counseling ministry. G4 and GCM affirm the unique value that both friendship and professional counseling provide. G4 and GCM leaders also recognize that their ministries exist between these two forms of care, and they remain compassionately but firmly within their roles.

PHASE SIX: ADD ADDITIONAL MINISTRIES THROUGH THE SAME PROCESS

As mentioned earlier, this six-phase process is cyclical. It is something you will repeat as your counseling ministry grows. If your church starts with GCM, it will go through this process again if it adds G4 (or vice versa). When you add new groups to your G4 ministry, you will go through an abbreviated version of this process to assess what unique needs the new group may present. For example, you would ask, "What resources need to be added to our next-level referral list for this new subject area?"

As your ministry grows, you will likely need to increase consultation hours. The more counseling your church provides, the more crises your church will be involved in. The more crises your church is involved in, the more worthwhile you will find this consultation expense. Eventually, the church may decide this consulting counselor role merits a staff position. If so, the job description will have written itself as you answer these two questions:

- What set of qualifications are needed to oversee the existing ministries well?
- What opportunities could be created if we had someone who could [fill in the blank]?

CONCLUSION

It's okay to admit that this chapter has required a lot of work. That's kind of how ministries grow. Vision-casting is exciting. Implementation is where things can get bogged down. But details matter. We don't want to invite people into the heightened vulnerability of counseling without having done the work necessary to steward those disclosures well.

If you understand and are prepared to move carefully through the phases we've just discussed, you are almost ready to launch your ministry. The remaining chapters of this book will be about making sure you launch *well* by assembling a strong support network of counselors in the community, communicating accurately with the congregation and community, and ensuring that your church leadership team fully understands and supports this new ministry.

Chapter 17

FROM REFERRAL LIST
TO COUNSELING CONSULTANT

In the previous chapter, we said having a referral list is important. But we focused on how having a good referral list gives confidence to volunteers and church leadership. Now we're going to consider how to develop a holistic referral list and crisis management response plan within your counseling ministry. We'll do that by answering these four questions:

1. How do you make a referral list?
2. How do you vet potential referral resources?
3. How do you know when to refer someone for outside help?
4. What is the role of your counseling consultant?

HOW TO MAKE A REFERRAL LIST

Creating a referral list requires making a series of phone calls, asking basic questions, and compiling the information gathered into an organized document. It takes time, but it's not complicated. You may choose to gather additional information—such as the credentials of each counselor and the insurance providers they accept—but the following chart shows the basic information you need to record.

Counseling Center	Counselor	Specialties	Phone Number	Website
Grace Counseling	Ann Smith	Children Depression Family Conflict	1.234.567.8912	web address
	Jaylen Doe	Addiction Chronic Pain		
Crossroads Counseling	Susan Davis	Eating Disorders Cutting	1.345.678.9123	web address
	Beth Revis	PTSD Depression Anxiety		
Hope Hospital Detox	n/a	Addiction Detox	1.456.789.0123	web address

When you call each counselor, conclude each conversation by asking who they recommend for needs that they are not equipped to counsel. If they claim to be competent for everything, be leery that they do not know their limits. Once you begin to hear only names that are already on your list, know you have a comprehensive list of the counseling options available in your community.

When giving a G4 or GCM participant a recommendation from this list, only copy–paste the name and contact information for the counselor or program that can best meet the individual's need. Do not send the entire document. You don't want to overwhelm the individual with options, and you want to show that you took time to personalize your recommendation to their need.

You may be wondering, *How can we know whether a given counselor's care is compatible with the Christian faith?* That is where we will turn our attention next.

HOW TO VET POTENTIAL REFERRAL RESOURCES

Vetting a potential counselor begins with asking questions and knowing why you are asking those questions. You won't ask every

counselor on your referral list every question. But for counselors who
(a) are excited about your ministry and seem like a viable option to
serve in a consulting role, or (b) meet a need that is otherwise absent
from your list, there are specific questions you want to ask.

The questions below assume the counselor with whom you are
speaking is a Christian and shows interest in learning about your
church's counseling ministry. This level of vetting goes beyond the
counselor's general competence and begins to explore unique ways
they may assist your ministry. Here are seven sets of questions to help
you vet a counselor as a referral resource.[1]

**1. What are your areas of specialty in counseling? What life
struggles do you not counsel?** No counselor is competent at everything. If a counselor cannot clearly and comfortably talk about subjects they are not equipped to handle, this should be a red flag. It
either means they are ill-experienced (not yet aware of the areas they
are not equipped to handle) or overly idealistic (convinced they are
competent in all matters).

As a counselor articulates their specialties and areas in which
they are not equipped to counsel, they are revealing where they
would best be able to serve your ministry. You are listening to identify
a good referral resource, but you are also listening to identify topics
for which this person might train your leaders.

**2. Why did you become a counselor? What do you enjoy about
it? What is the most difficult part of the profession?** Good counselors
can talk about what is rewarding and draining in their profession.
You want to assess how comfortably the counselor can talk about
unpleasant things (an important skill for counseling effectiveness). A
counselor whose answer is flat or nonengaging to a question like this
may be imagining having a purely business relationship with your
church, viewing it simply as a source of referrals.

**3. How did you come to faith in Christ, and what church are you
a member of?** The first part of getting to know what someone means

---

1. A version of this list was first created to help pastors vet potential referral resources
in their communities. The original version of this content can be found at "For Pastors:
How to Vet Potential Counseling Referral Sources," bradhambrick.com/vetcounselors.

by being a "Christian counselor" is getting to know what they mean by being a Christian. Listen for both how they came to faith and how they are continuing to mature spiritually. You are not looking for someone who is necessarily part of your same denomination, but you want to hear a clear understanding of the gospel and a commitment to growing in their personal faith.

The counselor who is enthusiastic in their response is a candidate to serve as your counseling consultant. You want someone in the consultant role who is not only clinically proficient, but also actively reflecting on the intersection of their faith and practice.

4. How do you approach moral guidance in counseling? How do you determine if a given individual's struggle is more rooted in sin or suffering? Often, when church leaders ask counselors whether they use the Bible in counseling, this is what they really want to know. A counselor's specializations may influence how a counselor answers this question. For example, a counselor who specializes in trauma is more likely to be focused on the suffering side of counseling. Counselors who can talk clearly about this question will understand the kind of categories brought to bear in a church's counseling ministry.

5. What do you view as the best and worst practices in relationships between counselors and local churches? This question sets up an opportunity for the two of you to discuss your best and worst experiences of relationships between counselors and churches. Each of you should share examples of what has worked or not worked as a way of establishing shared expectations for how you can work well together.

6. Who are your favorite Christian counseling authors? What book would you have me read? Let's face it, most church leaders love books and are always looking for a good recommendation. But beyond this, you will get a good feel for the approach of a counselor by reading the Amazon reviews on several books from their favorite authors and reading at least a few chapters from their favorite Christian counseling book.

7. As you come across good resources on [insert subject], can you send me links or recommendations? If you are pleased with the conversation to this point, this question can be a great way to end this conversation while extending the relationship. Have a list of the three to five most prevalent struggles faced by participants in your ministry. Ask the counselor to send you links to blog posts, podcasts, articles, or books they find relevant to these topics. A counselor who takes the time to do this shows you they are interested in serving your counseling ministry, not just having you as a referral source.

HOW TO KNOW WHEN TO REFER

We wish we could take life struggles and organize them on a T-chart like the one below.

Struggles for Lay or Pastoral Counseling	Struggles for Professional Counseling
1.	1.
2.	2.
3.	3.

This kind of chart would make life simpler. So why didn't I give you a chart like that? *When we think in terms of a T-chart, we add to the stigma and isolation commonly associated with counseling.* We inadvertently communicate that a person needs to fix their life and come back to church when they're better. But the person experiencing a life struggle that merits professional counseling still needs Christian friends, a pastor, and potentially a support group or mentor.

This means we need to rethink what it means to refer someone to a professional counselor. Unfortunately, *referral* has too often meant *hand off*. Without meaning to, a church says, "Your problem is too big for us. We can't help you." Instead, it is more God-honoring to think of a referral as adding someone to the team. In this case a church is saying, "You would benefit from someone with more expertise than we have. We will continue to fill our roles as pastor, friends, group leaders, or mentors, and care for you in those ways as you seek this additional care."

Garrett Higbee, in his book *Uncommon Community*, developed a version of the following chart to help churches identify when adding someone to the team would be advisable.[2] In this version, I have adapted the columns to correspond with the levels of care described in chapter 9.

- Level one is one-another care.
- Level two is the G4 and GCM ministries you are starting.
- Level four is the experienced professional level of care.
- Level three is omitted because that is the muddy middle that we said most churches are not equipped to do well.

	LEVEL 1 CARE	LEVEL 2 CARE	LEVEL 4 CARE
SEVERITY	**Friendship Care**	**G4 or GCM**	**More Experienced Care**
	Wisdom Issue	Moderate Conflict	Crisis
	Mild Stress	Distressed but Functioning	Stronghold Sin
	Everyday Problems	More Complex Issues	Significant Suffering
OWNERSHIP	**Friendship Care**	**G4 or GCM**	**More Experienced Care**
	Repentant	Sees Sin	Blame Shifts
	Open	Makes Excuses	Defensive
	Highly Teachable	Moderately Teachable	Denial—Not Teachable
SUPPORT	**Friendship Care**	**G4 or GCM**	**More Experienced Care**
	Close to Family	Some Family Support	Estranged from Family
	Intimate and Accountable	Few Friends	No Friends
	Vulnerable in Small Group	Somewhat Open in Small Group	Isolated—Not in Small Group

The three rows in this chart define three areas of assessment: (a) *the severity* of the life struggle, (b) *the level of ownership* over key

---

2. Modified and adapted with permission from Garrett Higbee, *Uncommon Community: Biblical Soul Care in Small Groups* (available at soulcareconsulting.com), 51.

choices, and (c) *the degree of social support* in the individual's life. The three columns provide descriptions that indicate a growing degree of concern: (a) column one describes a context in which a mature Christian friend should be able to provide adequate care, (b) column two describes a level where G4 and GCM serve well, and (c) column three describes situations for which the care of an experienced counselor is needed. This third column describes the situation of a mentee or group member that should prompt a lay leader to consult with the G4 or GCM director.

It's important to emphasize, though, that the levels of care in these three columns are not mutually exclusive. When level-two care is advisable, it provides optimal benefit when level-one care is also active. Similarly, when level four care is advisable, the support of level one and level-two care can increase its effectiveness. There is never a point where friendship is not beneficial, even when more experienced care is also warranted.

Do your lay leaders and pastors need to memorize this chart? No. Should they pull it out and walk through it with someone as they consider making a referral? Definitely not. Should they be familiar enough with this chart that it informs how they think about a distressed situation? Yes.

This chart gives words to what lay counseling leaders, like those in G4 and GCM, often sense when they feel in over their heads. Raising awareness of these categories lets your leaders know they will be supported when they recommend additional care because more is needed than they can provide.

JOB DESCRIPTION FOR YOUR COUNSELING CONSULTANT

Historically, a good relationship between churches and counselors has been difficult to forge. There are many reasons for this, but as we conclude this chapter, we will name and seek to alleviate one: *it is hard to reconcile the formal parameters of a counselor's helping relationships and the peer environment of local churches*. An understanding of the ethical parameters of each other's helping relationships should allow for a mutually satisfying consulting relationship between a church and a counselor.[3]

The challenge we're navigating reflects how each side understands the key word here: *ethics*. Church members who hear the word *ethics* think, *Don't sin*. Counselors hear the word *ethics*, and think, *Honor my professional code*. Both are legitimate uses of the word.

In this annotated job description, we will speak to both the counselor and church leadership. We will start with the counselor because the issues surrounding a church–counselor relationship have greater implications for their vocation. A counselor wants to make sure they don't get their licensed revoked.

The counselor, the G4 and/or GCM director, and the church leaders should discuss this job description as part of the process of deciding whether a consulting relationship will work for both parties. The final section of this job description lists additional topics you should discuss to make this decision.

JOB DESCRIPTION: COUNSELOR CONSULTANT FOR G4 AND/OR GCM MINISTRIES

To the Professional Counselor

- *This is **not** an LMHC-S or LMFT-S-esque relationship.* When you hear "counseling consultant," this is likely where your mind goes. You may need to describe to your church friends what that type of relationship is like and why you cannot agree to that style of arrangement with them.
- *You are **not** advising the helper, but the helper's director.* This is one reason this role is not an LMHC-S or LMFT-S-esque relationship. You are consulting with the G4 or GCM director, not the G4 group leader or GCM mentor about direct care. You should read the chapters introducing these ministries to understand the type of lay care being provided.

---

3. For more information on this, consider the article "Comparing Pastoral Ethics and Counseling Ethics" at bradhambrick.com/comparing-pastoral-ethics-and-counseling -ethics/.

- *You are **not** offering a diagnosis or diagnostic suggestions.* This is another reason this role is not an LMHC-S or LMFT-S-esque relationship. It would go beyond the scope of a church's training to try to give a diagnosis, and it would be unethical for you to suggest a diagnosis for someone who is not your direct client.

- *You **should** be familiar with the ethical guidance for G4 and GCM.* That means reading section two of this book. You may understand the implications of these three chapters more than your church friends do. Part of your role is advising them about operating these ministries within the guidelines provided.

- *You **are** ensuring wise triage.* We give a basic triage model in appendix A. When safety, addiction, trauma, or comparable factors need to be at the forefront of thinking through someone's care, your role is to help the G4 or GCM director see that these things must be given top priority and understand why that is so.

- *You **are** offering your awareness of community resources.* When higher-level triage needs exist, you know the resources in your community that can address these needs. We have already advised your church friends on creating a referral list. But you have the experience to coach them on which resource is the best fit and how to effectively recommend these resources to those who need them.

- *You **are** helping to identify the limits of peer-based care.* There are times when caring becomes enabling, or good intentions contribute to a problem more than alleviate it. In your consultation, if it becomes clear to you that this is happening in a G4 or GCM relationship, you should help the director see how this dynamic is emerging—for both the benefit of the participant and the longevity of the well-intended leader.

To Church Leadership

- *Honor the communication chain.* The only point of contact for the consultant is your G4 and/or GCM director. The counselor is not agreeing to consult on every pastoral care case in the church. Doing that would require them to have a staff position, not a consulting role. They are agreeing to consult with one or two specific ministries that have parameters which allow those ministries to work effectively with the ethical guidelines of the counselor's profession.

- *Do not name or quote the counselor to the person in distress.* The G4 or GCM director should never say, "I spoke to counselor, [name], about your situation and they think…" That would imply that the counselor is vicariously assessing an individual instead of advising the church about how to effectively oversee a ministry.

- *Do not name the individuals in distress.* It is enough to say, "We have a difficult situation with a 28-year-old male who is married and a father of two children under the age of seven." The counselor does not need personally identifying information to fulfill their role. It is better, in terms of helping the counselor honor their professional ethical code, not to have such identifying information.

- *If the counselor is a member of your church, protect their experience of church.* Don't have your consulting conversations before or after church services. Do not reference your counseling consultant on your church website. They offer direct care for twenty-five to thirty hours per week. If church becomes another place of direct care, it will be difficult for them to persevere in this role.

NEXT STEPS TO BE TAKEN TOGETHER

- *Discuss section two of this book together.* Chapters 13-15 are the ethical guidelines for G4 and GCM. Before most counselors will be willing to accept a consulting role, they will want to understand these parameters. Discussing this material together is vital to setting up a consulting relationship that will be mutually satisfying.

- *Review your launch plan from chapter 16 together*. This plan contains the specifics of what the counselor will be consulting about at your church. After discussing this job description, the ethical guidelines, and this plan, the church and counselor should be able to determine whether this will be a viable working relationship.

- *Decide on the initial frequency of interaction*. Consultation can either be episodic or on a set interval. Episodic implies "as needed" and is a good option when the ministry is small. A set interval might involve a weekly breakfast meeting or twice monthly phone calls.

- *Discuss the financial arrangement*. It is recommended that the church compensate the counselor at an hourly rate that is the equivalent of their hourly counseling fee. This allows the counselor to devote the time needed to adequately assist the church without negatively impacting their business or personal livelihood.

With these shared expectations and parameters, the church and the counselor should be able to establish a mutually satisfying consulting relationship. The church gains access to an experienced counselor who is familiar with the resources in their community and is able to advise on the difficult situations that will inevitably emerge. The counselor gets an opportunity to use their training and expertise to enhance the ministry of a local church in a way that is ethically wise and relationally sustainable.

Chapter 18

WHEN DO WE PUT A "COUNSELING" TAB ON THE CHURCH WEBSITE?

Putting a counseling tab on your church website tips many dominoes. Your ministry needs to be prepared to respond to the variety of inquiries before it takes the step of going public to that degree. For that reason, you may choose to start with a soft launch. A *soft launch* means G4 or GCM is active but not broadly promoted within the church or surrounding community.

During this phase G4 or GCM would only receive referrals from the pastoral staff and a few select ministries within the church. A soft launch can be a valuable time to work out communication kinks and allow lay leaders to get comfortable in their new roles. Don't rush through the benefits that come during a soft launch.

Eventually, you will want to go public with your counseling ministry. Putting a counseling tab on your church website is the most common way for a counseling ministry to go public. This is when you will initiate all of your promotion strategies within your church and surrounding community. When your counseling ministry goes public, you want as many people as possible to know about the care available.

As you think about creating a counseling page on your church website, have one idea at the forefront of your mind: *this page is an invitation*. The page will likely be the second point of contact after someone learns about your ministry from a church announcement, community referral, or other source. The purpose of your counseling page is to help people know where to be, what will happen, and how this ministry will serve them. You want it to be clear and welcoming.

We will approach this topic from two perspectives. First, what does this look like when your counseling ministry is in an organic, grassroots growth phase? Second, what does this look like when/if your decentralized counseling ministry coalesces into a centralized ministry or when your church launches G4 and/or GCM as a major new ministry initiative?

TWO GAUGES TO MONITOR

You are ready to create a counseling tab on your church website when

1. you have the *capacity* for new participants, and
2. you can *communicate clearly* about your ministry.

If during the soft launch you get near full capacity, don't put the ministry on your website yet. You don't want to flood a new ministry. If during the soft launch, you find participants are unclear about what this ministry is, hold off on going public. This is an indicator that you need to work on the clarity of your communication.

Drafting the website content well is important; make sure you concisely and clearly describe your *current* counseling ministry. Don't vision-cast about the *future* counseling ministry on the website. Only describe what you currently offer. If you are only implementing G4, then label the tab "counseling groups" instead of "counseling." Or if you use GCM only for premarital mentoring, don't use the words "marriage mentoring" on your website. Clarity cares for people by limiting confusion.

WEBSITE BASICS

First, let's consider an appropriate web address for the counseling page on your church's website. You want the ending of the link to reflect the ministry or ministries available at your church. If your church offers two or more counseling-related ministries, the link might be churchwebsite.com/counseling. If you offer only G4, it might be churchwebsite.com/G4. And if you offer only GCM, it might be churchwebsite.com/GCM.

Second, let's take a moment to consider a quick overview of the basic pieces of information your web page needs to include. Further explanations of some items on the following list appear in the sections to come:

- The name of the ministry or ministries
- The nature of the help offered
- The backgrounds and roles of the group facilitators and/or mentors
- The curriculum used
- The point of contact, whether a ministry director, a pastor, or a specific group facilitator (see the recommendations below)
- Clear instructions for how to join a group or be assigned a mentor
- The day, time, and length of the meeting(s)
- The location of the meeting(s)

As you begin creating content for your web page, you might find it helpful to refer back to the descriptions of G4 and GCM in chapters 3 and 5 of this book and to look at the examples of completed web pages at summitchurch.com/G4 and summitchurch.com/GCM.

Once your web page has gone live, be sure to keep it updated. If a group dissolves, for example, remove it from your list of available groups. And don't forget to send the web page link to the counselors on your referral list so they can recommend it to their clients.

WEBSITE GUIDANCE FOR DECENTRALIZED G4 GROUPS

A challenge for a ministry composed of decentralized groups—groups that meet on different nights of the week at different locations—is being clear about when and where each group meets. There is also the dilemma of deciding how to connect new participants with a group's leader prior to their first meeting.

It is recommended that you create a contact form that goes directly to the group leader rather than posting the leader's name and email address on the church's counseling page. Socially, you don't want your addiction group leader to become "the addiction person" at church. Leaders in your counseling ministry still need their church to be a place where they can have non-counseling peer relationships.

Provide group leaders with a copy–paste template that they can personalize to respond individually to each online inquiry. If your church has a G4 or GCM director, this person will also use comparable copy–paste replies for frequently asked questions. This ensures a degree of quality control over communications and limits the time burden on the group leader. A template email might look like this:

[Name],

Thank you for your interest in [Church's Name]'s G4 group on [topic]. I am the lay leader in our church that facilitates this group. We are excited about G4 and hope you will find it beneficial.

Here are answers to frequently asked questions about our group:

- **When and where does the group meet?** [day of the week, time, duration, location, and clear directions to meeting spot]
- **Do I need to purchase curriculum or is it provided?** [Explain whether your church sponsors the curriculum or has participants reimburse the church.]
- **Who is a part of this group?** Participants in the group are members of our church or community who are working to overcome [group topic].
- **What is the training level and role of the group leader?** G4 leaders are facilitators of their groups who have personal experience overcoming the focal topics. They are not professional counselors and do not provide individual counseling sessions.

- **What is expected of me?** Each participant is expected to put forth a good-faith effort by faithfully working through the curriculum and being honest about their successes and setbacks. Each participant is expected to be encouraging toward other members and keep the content of these conversations confidential.
- **How long am I committing to be a part of the group?** Each participant works through the curriculum at their own pace. You are welcome to participate in the group for as long as you find it beneficial.

If you need more clarity about one of these questions, I am happy to answer those via email. But for other questions, we could talk before or after group. G4 is a great place to find support and direction for a needed journey. We hope you will join us.

Notice that this template continues to answer the key questions of informed consent while establishing the role of a G4 leader as group facilitator, not personal counselor.

In a decentralized model, when group leaders handle the initial contact with new participants, it can be easy for an expectation of individualized care to emerge. For this reason, you also want to provide group leaders a template for responding to requests for individual guidance.

[Name],

I appreciate your [interest/participation] in G4. Our church is excited about the care these groups provide. My role and training are to facilitate the group. You raise important questions, but it is outside my role to provide individualized guidance. If you need guidance beyond what we cover in group discussion, I would be happy to connect you with a pastor for pastoral counseling or a professional counselor in our community. Again, I am grateful for your interest in our group and want to make sure you get connected with whatever supplemental care would benefit you.

G4 group leaders are not on-call counselors, life coaches, or crisis managers. If a group leader feels like such service is the church's expectation or allows a participant to push them into these roles, they will burn out. Having a church-endorsed, prewritten response helps leaders stay within their limits when questions go beyond what their role prepares them to answer.

WEBSITE GUIDANCE FOR CENTRALIZED G4 OR GCM MINISTRIES

When you centralize your counseling ministry, communication becomes more streamlined. Instead of having an addiction group that meets on Monday night at six o'clock, a women's depression group on Tuesday night at seven o'clock, and a grief group that meets on Friday nights at six thirty, you can simply say, "Our G4 groups meet on Tuesday nights at six thirty in the church's education wing. All active groups are listed at churchwebsite.com/G4."

For the pastoral team, church members, and community counselors to whom participants will sometimes be referred, this clarity is immensely beneficial. But once you get to this point, the counseling page will have more traffic and will serve as a connecting point to a greater variety of groups. For this reason, you'll need one designated contact person for all inquiries about the ministry.

We said above that your church's counseling web page is an invitation. To add a personal, welcoming touch, you may want to create a brief video featuring your G4 or GCM director describing the overall ministry. This introduces potential participants to whom they will hear from first and why.

Clarity is also key at multisite churches, where you may have multiple centralized G4 ministries meeting on different evenings and in different locations. For example, you may have one collection of G4 groups that meet on Monday nights at your North campus and a different collection of groups that meet on Thursday nights at your

Downtown campus. Go out of your way to make it obvious which groups meet at each location.

Monday Nights, North Campus, 6:30 p.m.	Thursday Nights, Downtown Campus, 6:30 p.m.
Current Groups* • Addiction (Coed) • Depression (Coed) • Men's Purity • Women's Purity • Trauma (Coed) • *GriefShare* (Coed) • Women's Eating Disorder * Please note these are the only active groups currently meeting at the North campus G4 ministry on Monday nights.	Current Groups** • Addiction (Coed) • Men's Purity • *DivorceCare* (Coed) • Men's Anger • Women's Betrayal (for wives affected by their husbands' adultery or sexual addiction) • Destructive Relationships (Coed; for those recovering from a relationship marked by abuse or addiction) ** Please note these are the only active groups currently meeting at the Downtown campus G4 ministry on Thursday nights.

The more your counseling ministries do, the clearer your communication must become. It might be easy to think the opposite: *The more our counseling ministry does, the more everyone will intuitively understand.* But that's not true. When you just offer a depression group, no one will think you also address eating disorders. But when you have groups for seven different topics, that changes.

It is easy for a counseling ministry that does lots of things to be talked about as if it does everything. You do not want well-meaning pastors or members telling people, "Just show up. They're awesome. They'll have just what you need." That is not good for the hopeful participant, and it is not good for your G4 leaders.

Once again, a tension arises from having a counseling ministry within a church. Most church gatherings are social gatherings. And for these gatherings, just showing up is great. Anyone can participate and hear, "We're so glad you've come." But a counseling ministry, even a groups-based ministry, is not a social gathering. In this sense, the counseling ministry is more like youth camp than like your weekly youth services. For youth services, anyone can show up. If we need more chairs, "Glory!" If we need more pizza, consider it ordered. For youth camp, however, we need parent permission slips, room reservations, and the proper adult to student ratios. As much as we want you to come, you can't just show up and get on the bus.

The first step to such clarity is having a clear counseling page on your church website. It provides a single source for accurate, up-to-date information. The second step is emphasizing in *every* public announcement about the counseling ministry the importance of checking the website for active groups.

Even if the pastor is preaching on grief and mentions G4 as part of the sermon, he should be in the habit of saying, "Please check churchwebsite.com/G4 for the other G4 groups we currently offer." This allows the relevance of one group (in this case, grief) to raise awareness for the entire G4 ministry without disrupting the flow of the sermon or giving inaccurate information.

CONCLUSION

Creating the counseling tab on your church's website is not about web design or aesthetic appeal. It is about *capacity* and *clarity*. Launch the counseling tab when your groups have the capacity for new participants and when you can clearly communicate what your ministry is and does. After that, your web page will become the primary hub for ensuring that anyone interested in your counseling ministry can get accurate, up-to-date information.

Chapter 19

FIVE CONVERSATIONS
WITH YOUR SENIOR PASTOR

hapter 19 is your cumulative final exam. It is not an exam where the pastor is the professor and the G4 or GCM director is the student. It is a mutual exam in which both of you are making sure you are on the same page. As you near launch phase, everyone (pastoral staff and lay leaders in the counseling ministry) should mean the same thing by the same words and have shared expectations for ministry that is about to happen. This chapter is about making sure all of those words and expectations are in sync.

SETTING THIS CONVERSATION UP FOR SUCCESS

Hopefully this section is not needed. But just in case it is, we'll cover it. If you are a layperson, have devoured this book, and are about to call your pastor for a first conversation about starting a counseling ministry, we probably need to do some expectation management. It may be that you are ready to christen a ship you believe is ready for its maiden voyage, and your pastor will want to begin the process of assessing the vessel to make sure it's seaworthy.

Remember the ground we covered regarding liability and clarifying what counseling means. You have become comfortable and proficient with these concepts. In a first conversation, your pastor probably won't be. More than one conversation has gone off the rails when an excited church member pitched an idea to an unsuspecting pastor. The conversation goes off the rails not because the pastor is resistant, but because the pastor has liability or procedural concerns he isn't sure how to articulate or assuage.

Our final exam has five questions to consider. If this is your pastor's first exposure to the possibility of a counseling ministry, expect these questions to be discussed over several different conversations. However, if you and your pastor have already been talking about starting a counseling ministry, these questions should feel like an open-book exam. These conversations are an opportunity for the two of you to reflect together on how much you've learned and to pray over the final stages of your launch.

With that said, here are your **five final exam questions** to discuss:

1. What do we mean by "counseling"?
2. What are we initially offering?
3. Do we have our next-level referrals and consultant?
4. Is the church's insurance provider aware of our plan?
5. When and how do we launch?

Question 1: What do we mean by "counseling"?

Imagine a member hears that the church is launching a counseling ministry and asks, "How do I get an appointment with a counselor?" What is your response?

As you think through your response, recognize that it's not bad for someone to misunderstand what your counseling ministry is. They're not being resistant or undermining. They're guessing. You need to be able to clarify what your counseling ministry is without being defensive or seeming annoyed.

If your church is launching both GCM and G4, you might give an answer like the one below. If you are only launching one or the other, you would only respond with the pieces that fit what your church is currently offering.

Thank you for your interest in our counseling ministry. The ministry consists of counseling groups and premarital mentoring. With that said, we don't have "counselors" to make an appointment with, but groups you can attend. An up-to-date list of the current groups can always be found at churchweb site.com/counseling. If none of these groups meets your need, you could meet with a pastor for pastoral counseling, or we can recommend a professional counselor in our community.

Having read chapter 9, you should be able to pick up on how this answer conversationally describes the difference between level-three or level-four counseling (how the member used the word "counseling" in their request) and level-two counseling (what your church offers). If what you currently offer is not a match for what someone needs, the work you did in preparing to launch your counseling ministry prepares you to connect them with a counselor that is a good fit.

Question 2: What are we initially offering?

In this book we've talked about a wide variety of subjects that you *could* address using the G4 and GCM models. Vision-casting is fun. But now it's time to get narrow and decide where to start. Once your initial offerings are running well, you can begin envisioning new opportunities again.

Chances are your answer to question two is shorter than you would like. It doesn't touch on everything we brainstormed together. Don't let that discourage you. Do these first things well, and the ministry will grow.

Starting a ministry is more like building a house than drawing a house. You can draw a house quickly, but a picture provides no shelter. It takes longer to build a house, but it can be a source of refuge to many. The work you've done to this point is like building a house; as you continue to add to it, this ministry will become a source of refuge for more people.

Question 3: Do we have our next-level referrals and consultant?

Question two pushes us to ask question three. If our counseling ministry doesn't do everything (which it never will) and having a counseling ministry is going to invite more requests for help, then we need points of connection for additional care.

Even if your answer to question two was not as robust as you wanted, realize you are now more equipped to connect members of your church with good care. Having a counseling ministry invites questions that previously remained unspoken. That silence meant people were hurting alone. You are making a big difference even when your counseling ministry starts small.

Question 4: Is the church's insurance provider aware of our plan?

The answers to questions one, two, and three set you up to answer the questions that will emerge when your pastor calls the church's insurance provider. If possible, the G4 and/or GCM director should participate in this conversation. Your insurance provider will want to know what your church means by "counseling," what your church is going to offer, and what you plan to do with needs that go beyond what you offer.

Here are two statements and two questions to discuss with your church's insurance provider. As you can see, statement one assumes that your church is launching both G4 and GCM; once again, you can adapt the model given here to fit the ministry your church plans to offer.

Two statements:
1. We plan to begin a group-based counseling ministry and a premarital mentoring ministry. Comparable equivalents to the group-based ministry would be Alcoholics Anonymous, Celebrate Recovery, or Stephen's Ministry.
2. The leaders in this ministry are laypeople who volunteer their time (like small group leaders or lay elders who offer pastoral care) and not credentialed counselors (licensed mental health professionals). We'll clarify this at each point in the ministry entry process.

Two questions:
1. What additional coverage, if any, do we need, and what will it cost?
2. At what thresholds of growth would this coverage need to be updated? For example, if we had fifteen groups with an

average of 150 participants per week, would the coverage need to increase?

Question 5: When and how do we launch?

Now you're getting to the nitty-gritty: names and dates and times. In this conversation with your pastor—and any others who are part of getting this ministry underway—you are working toward being able to give concrete answers to each of the following questions:

- What is its official first meeting date?
- For G4
  - » Who is the G4 director?
  - » What night of the week do groups meet?
  - » Where do groups meet?
  - » Who responds to inquiries about groups?
  - » To whom do G4 leaders report?
  - » To whom does the G4 director report?
- For GCM
  - » Who is your mentor coordinator?
  - » To whom does the mentor coordinator report?

When you start discussing the above questions, you may not be at the ready-to-launch phase of development. The good thing about this final exam is that you can take all the time you need to complete it well. But in this exam, you can't leave any answers blank. These are all questions that will need to be answered before you officially begin your ministry.

Hopefully, based on the effort you've put in to get to this point, these questions are less overwhelming than they would have been when you began this book. You have done the hard work of understanding the principles on which a counseling ministry is built and the infrastructure that is required to run it well. You see the wisdom in knowing the limitations of your new ministry, but you also have a clearer vision of the ways it will serve individual participants, the church, and the wider community. Given all that you've learned, launching a counseling ministry can be exciting, rather than intimidating.

Appendix A

TRIAGE: WHERE TO BEGIN
IN COMPLEX SITUATIONS

In life and counseling, finding the starting point can be difficult. Life is fluid enough that identifying where to begin with tackling a life-dominating struggle can feel like finding the beginning of a circle. To help G4 and GCM leaders with this important question, we have provided a five-level triage model.

1. Safety
2. Addiction
3. Trauma
4. Character
5. Skill

The premise of this triage model is that if upper-level concerns exist, efforts at changing lower-level concerns are unlikely to be effective. Each participant is advised to start by addressing the highest-level concern that is present in their life.

Sometimes there is a connection between the higher- and lower-level issues a person is facing. A lower-level struggle may be a contributing cause to a higher-level struggle. For example, someone who is suicidal (level one—safety concern) may need to learn to manage their finances better (level five—skill concern) because pending bankruptcy fuels their hopelessness. This individual needs to be stabilized before they are able to implement a debt-reduction plan. Similarly, a person with a substance abuse problem (level two—addiction concern) may have anger management issues (level four—character concern), but until the abuse of a mind- or mood-altering substance is removed, attempts at learning emotional regulation will be short-lived.

In G4, this triage model helps the leader discern if a participant is in the right group and whether a participant needs to be meeting with an experienced counselor in addition to attending the G4 group. For instance, the person with both substance abuse and anger management issues may have joined a G4 group for anger management. But when the leader of the anger management group discovers that this person has substance abuse issues, they will know that the person needs to switch to the group for those struggling with addiction.

For GCM leaders, this triage model helps mentors discern when a couple has moved from marriage preparation or marriage enrichment level care (what GCM provides) to needing marriage restoration care (which is beyond the scope of GCM mentoring).

Note: The discussion below of each level of this triage model provides two sample response statements that illustrate what it might sound like to redirect a participant to address a higher-level concern. These responses simply redirect a participant to see the higher-level concern; any advice on the best context for continued care would be determined in discussion with the counseling consultant.

LEVEL ONE: SAFETY

When the basic requirements of safety are not present, safety takes priority over any other concern. Safety is never an unfair expectation from a relationship. If safety is a concern, then you should immediately involve appropriate authorities (legal authorities, CPS, or the parents of a minor). *This would be a time to contact the consultant you've contracted with to learn who the appropriate authority is and to avoid making the report in a way that further compromises safety.*[1]

This category includes thoughts of suicide, physical or sexual abuse, threats of violence (to people or pets), and similar actions. Until safety is no longer in doubt, other concerns should only be addressed

---

1. Additional guidance on the initial response to instances of abuse can be found at churchcares.com.

as a way of understanding how to create a safe disposition or environment for the individual.

> **Sample Response:** "I hear you talking about how hard it is for you to live realizing the pain you've caused your family. It makes sense why that is overwhelming, and I think it is important for us to discuss how to process the shame and despair you feel. But I want to make sure our conversation does not add to your sense that life is not worth living. Can we pause the conversation about what happened and what you fear having to do about it to remember why suicide is not an answer?"

> **Sample Response:** "I can tell you're upset about the ways you believe your wife disrespects you, but in describing it, you've mentioned several things that are concerning: striking her face when she back talked, not allowing a conversation to end when she asked for a break, and not allowing her to have access to transportation or her parents. These behaviors are abusive. They raise concerns of safety, which supersede concerns of disrespect. The way you describe her actions as 'causing' (and by implication 'excusing') your actions indicates that your lack of self-control is a greater concern than the relational differences in your marriage."

Note: While you are likely to contact your counseling consultant on level two through five concerns as well, safety level concerns should be a reason you seek consultation. The complexity of these situations and the number of variables that impact identifying the wisest next steps, make consultation with an experienced counselor essential.

LEVEL TWO: ADDICTION

After safety, the misuse of mind- or mood-altering substances is the next level of priority. This category includes alcohol, illegal drugs, prescription drugs not used according to instructions, and similar activities. Substance abuse inhibits any maturation process. The consistency and stability required for lasting change are disrupted by substance abuse.

On this same level would be a persistent pattern of self-destructive behaviors despite negative life consequences, even if that pattern does not involve a mind-altering substance. For instance, problematic gambling, chronic rudeness leading to repeated job loss, and other persistent, harmful behavior patterns fall into this category.

> **Sample Response:** "It is good that you want to learn how to manage conflict better, but when you've described your arguments, they usually happen when you've been drinking. It seems you have a drink most nights, and this leads to much of the conflict with your spouse. Several times you've blamed what you've said on having too much to drink. It is doubtful that you will practice the self-control necessary to engage conflict well if you continue to abuse alcohol. For this reason, if you are serious about improving your marriage, you will be willing to address your substance abuse problem."

> **Sample Response:** "I admire the courage you show in wanting to learn how to handle the emotions associated with losing your child in a traffic accident. The fear, anxiety, anger, and confusion you describe are very understandable. But it concerns me how much you are using alcohol to cope with this experience. One of the effects of escaping emotions through alcohol is that it stunts our ability to process such painful experiences. An important part of processing this experience healthily will be to forego the coping mechanism of alcohol."

LEVEL THREE: TRAUMA

Trauma is often evidenced by past or present events resulting in nightmares, sleeplessness, flashbacks, a sense of helplessness, restricted emotional expression, difficulty concentrating, persistent high levels of anxiety, intense feelings of shame, or a strong desire to isolate.

This category includes past physical or sexual abuse, verbal or emotional abuse, exposure to an act of violence, an experience of a disaster, a major loss, or similar experiences.

Sample Response: "I hear you talking about the changes in your marriage and job satisfaction over the last year. I cannot help but notice how that correlates with when you lost your father, whom you mentioned being very close to. You also mentioned how busy the time around his death was because you were responsible to administrate his will. It seems you may have started being strong because you had to (which meant ignoring and turning off your emotions), and now you're struggling to feel anything for your spouse or job. I think it would be unwise to make any decisions in those areas until you allow yourself to grieve the loss of your father."

Sample Response: "I admire your desire to become a more positive person and your willingness to acknowledge how your pessimism may be impacting your children. But what you're calling 'being negative' or 'anxiety' seems to be hypervigilance—a natural response to a trauma, like what happened when you lost everything in the house fire last year. I believe the most effective way to shape your character in the way you desire is to understand the impact of the trauma you and your children went through, so that you do not try to 'just be stronger' in a way that makes your normal response to a tragedy seem like a moral defect in your character."

LEVEL FOUR: CHARACTER

Character refers to the persistent values that express themselves in a variety of settings and in a variety of choices. Poor character is more than a skill-level problem. Character concerns reveal what we value most. For example, when someone stops yelling at their family when they answer the phone, this reveals a character problem. They are capable of self-control—as demonstrated by their composure on the phone—but their actions reveal that their reputation (one thing of value) is worth more to them than their family's well-being (a second thing of value). This is a character-level problem because it does not adhere to God's prioritization of these values.

Skill training alone will not change character. Character issues include angry outbursts, bitterness, some forms of fear, greed, jealousy, controlling tendencies, hoarding, envy, laziness, selfishness, use of pornography, codependency, insecurity, and similar things.

When character concerns exist, teaching skills without addressing an individual's beliefs and values results in change that only lasts as long as the consequences for misbehaving are present (in the example above, public awareness of their harshness). Character change happens when the change is maintained in the absence of imminent consequences.

> **Sample Response:** "It's great that you recognize how over-committed you are and how that leads to lying to your friends. I know you're seeking help with time management, but learning how to be more efficient with your time is only going to help if you are willing to tell people no. I wouldn't actually be helping you by teaching you how I approach projects. I think it would be better for us to discuss how I handle the possibility of disappointing people."

> **Sample Response:** "It takes a great deal of courage to admit you need to become a less controlling person. But the kinds of questions you're asking center on the 'rules of relationship'—what it is reasonable to expect from others without being considered controlling. Your expectations of what a friend should be are excessive. And even when your expectations are reasonable, when others disappoint you, you tend to overreact. You don't need better rules you can impose on your friends; you need to change your unrealistic expectations of others so that you can enjoy friendship with imperfect people more."

LEVEL FIVE: SKILL

With skill-level changes, the person is usually self-aware that change is needed. They want to learn the necessary skills and aren't defensive about the learning process. This category includes conflict resolution, time management, budgeting, planning, and similar skills. The sample responses for this section will have a different tone. They assume the individual is aggrandizing their life struggle (ranking it higher) instead of minimizing it (ranking it lower).

> **Sample Response:** "I can understand why you are upset with yourself for frequently being late and upsetting your friends. It's good that you're willing to address this pattern, but I'm not sure it means you're an abusive person or chronic liar. It seems that you're an extrovert who gets so lost in one moment that you lose any sense of what's next. If this is accurate, then we can begin by learning some scheduling or time management techniques. If this resolves the problem, then this is just a strength/weakness of your personality of which you need to be more aware and manage better."

> **Sample Response:** "I hear your concern that, as a parent, your anxiety may be negatively affecting your children. But you've described how your children feel safe bringing their fears to you. You seem to be able to enjoy playing with your children and allowing them to take appropriate risks in their play. For these reasons, I think it is sufficient for me to help you identify outlets to discuss and address your anxieties so that you are not ruminating on them in isolation." [In this case, the parent's struggle was remedied by a skill-level intervention of being more open with friends to prevent rumination.]

SUMMARY

As you start a counseling ministry, these are the kinds of conversations you and your leaders need to be prepared to have. Counseling begins with assessment: gauging the degree of the problem and what is most important.

The G4 and GCM curriculums facilitate these conversations by providing assessment tools early in each study. But these assessments will not remove the necessity of responses like the ones modeled above because people don't always accurately assess where they should start. For instance, someone may come to an anger group when their outbursts are better understood as expressions of trauma. This triage model gives the anger group leader a compassionate way to say, "I really appreciate your desire to grow, but here's why I think a different group would serve you better."

The challenges that accompany safety, addiction, and trauma level concerns reveal once again why it is important to have an experienced counselor consulting with your counseling ministry. These issues often involve complicating factors where the advisement of an experienced counselor can ensure participants are well cared for and leaders have peace of mind.

Appendix B

G4 SERIES NINE-STEP CURRICULUMS

While a G4 ministry can and is highly encouraged to utilize group-based counseling curriculum from other authors,[1] this appendix lists the G4 nine-step curriculum options and links to the video-based presentations of this content. Having several groups utilizing these curriculums helps participants understand why the elements of your opening G4 "big group time" are structured as they are. (The layout of an evening of G4 is discussed in *Facilitating Counseling Groups*.)

Note: After the publication of *Mobilizing*, each G4 curriculum will be published progressively by New Growth Press. Until a published edition of each curriculum is available, a printable PDF version will be available and can be requested at the links below.

False Love
*For chronic struggle with pornography,
sexual addiction, and adultery*
www.bradhambrick.com/falselove

---

1. A list of potential curriculums is available at "24 Possible Curriculum for a G4 Ministry," bradhambrick.com/G4curriculum. In addition, chapter 15 of *Facilitating* contains further guidance on vetting and selecting curriculums that do not use the G4 nine-step models.

True Betrayal

For the spouse of someone engaged in a chronic struggle with pornography, sexual addiction, and adultery

www.bradhambrick.com/truebetrayal

Overcoming Addiction

For substance-related addiction, although it could be used as a separate group for behavior addictions like gambling

www.bradhambrick.com/addiction

Navigating Destructive Relationships

For someone navigating the aftermath of a relationship marked by addiction or abuse

www.bradhambrick.com/destructive

Post-Traumatic Stress

www.bradhambrick.com/ptsd

Disordered Eating

For individuals struggling with overeating or restricting, but handled in different groups

www.bradhambrick.com/healthy

Overcoming Depression-Anxiety[2]

www.bradhambrick.com/depression

Overcoming Anger

www.bradhambrick.com/anger

---

2. The emotions of depression and anxiety are addressed as one topic because the co-occurrence rate of these emotions is so high. For severe struggles with either emotion (for example, suicidal ideation or acute phobias), G4 alone would not be an adequate form of care. This group would, at most, be supplemental care for individuals with severe struggles with only one of these emotions.